My Heart Got Married
And I Didn't Know It

To Evelyn —
From our hearts to yours ♥
Love Cloke
Barbara M Priscott

My Heart Got Married
And I Didn't Know It

Unspoken Vows and Shattered Dreams

Lora C. Jobe, BSN
Barbara U. Prescott, PhD

RESOURCE *Publications* · Eugene, Oregon

MY HEART GOT MARRIED AND I DIDN'T KNOW IT
Unspoken Vows and Shattered Dreams

Resource Publications
A Division of Wipf and Stock Publishers
199 W. 8th Ave., Suite 3
Eugene, OR 97401
www.wipfandstock.com

ISBN 13: 978-1-60608-635-3

Manufactured in the U.S.A.

*This book is lovingly dedicated to
our families.*

*Sarah, Dan, Naomi, and Fay
Lisa and Rob
Mark, Jr.*

*Allie
Allie IV and Allison*

Contents

Acknowledgments

THERE ARE MANY PEOPLE to thank for their support, encouragement, and kindness during the writing and publishing of our book.

First, of course, are our families. To Sarah, Lisa, and Mark, Jr. for your never-ending enthusiasm about the phenomenon of *heart marriage* and for your unwavering belief that the book would get published.

To Allie, a wonderful husband, friend and unbridled cheerleader, who is a constant source of love and strength. To Allie IV and Allison whose sweet encouragement and sincere approval of the book's message felt like the highest praise.

To the folks at Rutba House in Durham, North Carolina, especially Jonathan Wilson-Hargrove, who listened and asked questions about the concept early in the writing, you are loved and appreciated.

There were a few trusted readers along the way who kept us focused on telling the stories— Mimi Vestal, Barbara Ricks, Macon Ivy, Lyn and Tom Everett, Gloria Brown, and Dianne Homra.

Our appreciation goes to Ellen Pruitt, a fellow author, who shared her experience and gave us fortuitous tips that helped tremendously in the early going.

Thank you to Angela Petty, a beautiful young woman whose personal response to the concept of *heart marriage* even before the book was completed gave us confidence that it could positively impact lives. And to Jessica Skidmore, who requested and read a couple of chapters and said, "These women are telling my story and they don't even know me." Your candor motivated and humbled us.

We thoroughly enjoyed the copyediting process and owe a debt of gratitude to Nancy Shoptaw, who did an excellent job editing while gently challenging us to tighten the work.

Many thanks to Teresa Bullock who did graphic design work along the way.

To our book club friends, Les Belles Lettres, you kept us laughing! You are the best!

To Charlie Chilton, Amy Mendzela, Kathy Bucy, Emily Turner and the many other friends and family who go unnamed, thank you for being with us on this journey and for your smiles, hugs, emails, prayers and ideas. You are all so dear to us.

Introduction

MY LIFE EXPERIENCES OF fifty-plus years have revealed certain traits about the human heart. As Woody Allen said, "The heart wants what the heart wants" (Isaacson, "The Heart," last paragraph).

As a young woman, I watched a friend struggle in an on and off again relationship with a man who was not right for her. They had started dating very young, about age fifteen, had quickly become sexually intimate, and continued to date throughout high school. They broke up several times during college, but the breakups were so painful that they would reunite. During these years, her sisters and friends married. Eventually, after dating for fifteen years, the couple married. Within a year, they were divorced. Lots of folks were surprised. After all, they had dated for years, lived together for some of those years, and couldn't seem to live without each other. What I came to understand was that what they had needed all along was a divorce, but because they had never legally married, there was no mechanism for the unbinding of their hearts.

Over the years, I saw more than a few friends and acquaintances struggle through intimate, long term relationships that finally culminated in marriage only to be dissolved in a year or two by divorce. As cohabiting became more common in the 1980s and 90s, increasing numbers of young couples chose to live together to avoid the complications and responsibilities of marriage until they felt more prepared. What they didn't know was that their hearts would get married anyway, and if the relationship fell apart, the breakup would be every bit as wrenching as a divorce. This painful dissolution would occur without the words to define it or the support systems in place to work through it.

I began to share ideas about this phenomenon with my coauthor who is a professional therapist. She confirmed that she had seen many couples for marriage counseling who reported that they had misgivings about their relationship and knew before the wedding that something was wrong and that they should not marry. These couples had usually been sexually intimate, dated for a long time, and many had lived with each other. As a result, they often felt compelled to "go through with the marriage." Just as I had personally observed, she said that it began to appear to her that the couples, without realizing it, had to get married in order to get a proper divorce.

We are living in a time that has been described as the "Post-Sexual Revolution." The cultural norms and behaviors of couples have shifted and yet we have not fully explored the implications and fallout of these changes. This book is an effort to describe the phenomenon of *heart marriage* and *heart divorce* and how to avoid the pain and devastation that can result. Although unnamed, this phenomenon has been around for a long time. However, with the increase in cohabitation and the loosening of a traditional view of marriage, more and more couples are at risk of falling prey to *heart marriage*. Being able to name and recognize the signs of such a relationship, as well as see a viable way out, will hopefully enable more couples to make better decisions so that they can enjoy the benefits of a healthy marriage.

Lora C. Jobe

Heart Marriage and Heart Divorce

Unspoken Vows and Shattered Dreams

ALICE AND JAMES

ALICE WAS A RAVEN-HAIRED beauty who made A's through high school and college. At a prestigious university she excelled academically and was involved in student government. She was active in a human rights organization and sought ways to make the world a better place. Alice met James during their freshman year at a school mixer. James came from a wealthy southern family and was a solid student. He was socially comfortable and was usually the life of the party. When he and Alice began dating, they seemed to perfectly complement one another. He softened her type A driving ambition, and she enlightened him about world affairs. They dated throughout college, became sexually intimate, and talked about a future together. Upon graduation, they attended several weddings of college friends but did not feel this was the time for them to get married. Alice applied to graduate schools and was accepted everywhere she applied. James wasn't sure what he wanted to do, so he planned to work for a couple of years while exploring his options. The two moved to Nashville where she could pursue a graduate degree and he could work in business with some longtime family friends. They discussed living together, but decided against it for the time being. They also discussed marriage and generally felt they would marry after graduate school.

While they maintained separate apartments, James spent most nights with Alice. They ate dinner together, went out with mutual friends, vacationed with their families, and traveled together in Europe. It seemed natural that they would marry after several years together, but there always seemed to be a reason to wait. Alice wanted James to get serious about his career and to find a cause that would excite and motivate him to volunteer in the community. James wanted Alice to relax a little bit more. They each considered breaking off the relationship, but after all the years of dating, that option felt horrifying. Neither one of them could imagine starting over with someone else.

After seven years together, Alice had her Masters in Social Work and was hired at a respected nonprofit agency. James had a position doing consulting work. At his father's urging and with his mother's advice, he planned a trip to New England to ask Alice to marry him. James knew Alice wanted a perfect experience, from the proposal to the engagement to the wedding ceremony and reception. At a cozy bed and breakfast, he proposed and gave her a two-carat diamond ring that had been his great grandmother's. They began planning a huge society wedding that would take place over the course of a weekend at a luxury resort. The planning would take a year and a half.

During their engagement, they found a cute house in a great neighborhood and decided to buy it and move in together. Alice was frequently distracted with her demanding career and the wedding details, and she found that James often irritated her, as he did not seem to understand the amount of work involved in planning a wedding of this magnitude. James found himself fantasizing about other women and wishing Alice would agree to elope. They both pushed through these thoughts and rationalized that this was just a difficult time and that things would be better once they got married.

After the wedding, which was a very elaborate and special occasion, the couple honeymooned in the British Virgin Islands. They relaxed, enjoyed sex, which had been on the wane for the last year or so, and talked about the future. James was surprised and a bit bewildered when Alice suggested he find a more challenging job, with better opportunities for advancement. And Alice was aggravated when James said he would like to start a family and that maybe it was time for Alice to quit her volunteer work in the evenings.

Over the next few months, they had bitter arguments over the division of labor in the house and their lack of agreement on starting a family. When Alice broached the subject of a return to school to get her PhD, James left and spent the night with a friend. This one night separation shocked them into going to marriage counseling. After several sessions, they both realized that they did not see a future together. James moved into an apartment and Alice went to an attorney. They were devastated and heartbroken, but realized that for many years they had not acknowledged their growing differences. Friends and family were bewildered when their divorce was final before their second anniversary. *What happened?*

Alice and James are just one example of a phenomenon that we will call *heart marriage. A heart marriage is a relationship in which the couple is intimately bound together and practices the behaviors of marriage without the intentional and articulated agreement between both parties to marry.* Marriage, on the other hand is the intentional, intimate, and legal union of a man and woman who become husband and wife.

Long before Alice and James stood before the minister at the altar, they were married in many of the traditional ways and were bound together because of them. They dated exclusively and had an intimate sexual relationship for many years. Their living arrangement looked very much like a marriage, with shared living spaces and involvement in each other's daily activities. Both families accepted their relationship and treated them like a married couple. By mimicking all the behaviors of marriage, their hearts had become married, but they did not realize that is what had happened.

Before legally marrying, the idea of breaking up was very painful to Alice and James. They would grieve for the lost future they had imagined together and be gripped by the fear of being alone and lonely. These feelings were so wrenching and their separations so difficult that the two concluded they should be together. So they got married. Once they were married, there was a word to describe that kind of painful separation and that word is divorce. If Alice and James had been able to recognize that their hearts were married and that the hurt involved in splitting is comparable to getting a divorce, they would have been better prepared to negotiate the difficult work of separation at that time.

Everyone recognizes and understands that divorce is often devastating to the parties involved and to their families and friends. There should be a way to describe the painful process when a *heart marriage* is dissolving so that it too can be recognized and understood. This dissolution can best be described as a *heart divorce*. *A heart divorce is simply the formal, clearly articulated and agreed upon dissolution of a heart marriage.* The emotions of a *heart divorce* are very similar to those of a legal divorce. The sense of loss, depression, and heartbreak is as real as when a legal marriage is dissolved. By labeling what is happening, the couple is better able to acknowledge, discuss, and understand their feelings. Their support systems, such as family, friends, and professionals, also can understand more clearly the severity of the emotional response, which enables them to offer the kind of support needed by the couple.

Several things have happened in our society in the last fifty years that have changed sexual behavior and attitudes. First, with the advent of the birth control pill in the late 1960s and the risk of pregnancy minimized, sexual intimacy before marriage has become more common and acceptable. Additionally, with more educational and professional options available, women began to delay marriage. Finally, with the delay in marriage, it is increasingly common for couples to live together before marriage for a number of reasons. Couples who are already having sex and are together constantly say that it makes financial sense to live together. They may want to "try out" marriage by cohabiting before plunging into a legal marriage. Frequently, the couple does plan to marry at some time in the future but often the dreams and plans for the future have not been fully discussed and the couple assumes the details of their life can be worked out later.

The danger with any of these scenarios—prolonged dating, premarital sex, and cohabitation—is that the heart makes an attachment; *heart marriage* occurs; and the participants are not even aware that there has been a shift in the relationship. Friends of the couple may even say, "They act like a married couple." Well, indeed they do, because in fact, their hearts are married. This is dangerous because marriage, with all its difficulties, needs to be an intentional, mutually agreed upon commitment. The occurrence of *heart marriage* usually happens without the stated desire to be married at that time, normally because one or both parties is not ready to make that commitment. Thus, the dilemma is that a marriage has taken place without the full agreement of the participants.

A happy marriage is a sought after situation, as evidenced by the millions of married folks and the many divorced or widowed people who seek to be married again. At its best, the marriage partnership can make life infinitely happier and healthier. A quick review of the many "how to have a happy marriage" books and articles reveals list after list of ingredients necessary for a successful marriage. Those lists include things like unconditional love, commitment, ability to solve conflicts, willingness to compromise, sacrifice, and many more. Almost universally, though, the books and articles list honest and open communication as vital to maintaining a joyous marriage. Because *heart marriage* happens either before or without the stated intention to be married, there is a critical gap in communication that usually gets worse over time. This presents a problem for the health of the relationship in the long term. To have the fullness of marriage, *heart marriage* is not enough and can actually set up dishonest, confusing behavior patterns that get in the way when a true intentional marriage commitment is desired.

There are four indicators that help identify the occurrence of *heart marriage*. They are: sexual intimacy, monogamy, cohabitation, and reluctance to marry over time. These four indicators often appear sequentially starting with sexual intimacy. Then the relationship becomes monogamous. Cohabitation may or may not follow, but finally there is the reluctance to marry over time. If we think about Alice and James in light of these indicators, you will notice that all four are present in their relationship. They dated each other exclusively from the time they met in college and were sexually intimate. They did not officially live together until becoming engaged, but spent many nights together, effectively cohabiting. Their relationship certainly was prolonged, stretching from the first date as college freshmen into a period of nearly eight years before the wedding actually occurred. Finally, although early in their relationship they spoke of a future together and continued to assume it would happen at the appropriate time, as the years passed, there was a growing reluctance to make that final commitment. In their case, Alice and James didn't consciously own their feelings of reluctance, rather they found many concrete, and on the surface, reasonable excuses to delay marriage.

In the next chapter, we will look at a brief overview of these four indicators. Afterward, each indicator will be explored more closely in the order in which it typically occurs in the relationship. This insight will help us to understand how each has a binding effect on the heart and, in combination, can create this emotional dynamic that we call *heart marriage*. Before getting too far along in the book, you may want to take the Heart Marriage Quiz below to help determine if you or someone you know and care about may already be heart married.

HEART MARRIAGE QUIZ: ARE YOU HEART MARRIED?

Directions: Answer yes or no to the following questions about your relationship.

1. When talking about you and your girl/boyfriend, do people ever say, "You two act like a married couple"?

2. Do your friends often ask you when you and your boy/girlfriend are getting married and you feel a little uneasy about the question, either having many excuses or no answer at all even though you have been together for a long time?

3. Do you find yourself thinking that maybe this Christmas, birthday, or Valentine's your boyfriend will give you an engagement ring, and it never seems to happen?

4. Do you ever think about breaking up with your girl/boyfriend, but don't because you feel like you have invested so much time already or you are afraid of being lonely and starting over with someone else?

5. Have you had thoughts of ending your relationship or tried to break up but it's just too painful when you are apart, so you get back together, thinking that since you were so miserable, it must mean that you love each other and should be together?

6. Does sex seem to be the one thing that gets you and your partner through your difficulties and/or doubts about your relationship?

7. Do you ever have the feeling of being "stuck" in your relationship— that it's just rolling along to nowhere—and you wonder where all the years have gone and how you got to where you are?

8. Have you ever thought to yourself, "We've been together so long, I guess we ought to just go ahead and get married"?

9. When you make plans such as to take a trip or move to another city or even to buy a house, do you most always think in terms of you and your boy/girlfriend instead of just yourself?

10. Are at least two of the following four statement true of your relation-
     ship? a) You have been dating each other exclusively for more than
     a year and would feel like you were cheating if you dated someone
     else. b) You have been sexually intimate since fairly early in your
     relationship. c) You live together or practically live together with
     clothes and toothbrushes at each other's place. d) You have no stated
     or concrete plans to marry.

Scoring Key

♥   If you answered yes to five questions, it is possible you are heart
married.

♥   If you answered yes to eight questions, you are definitely heart
married.

♥   If you answered yes to question number ten and only one other
question, you are in danger of becoming heart married.

TAKING IT TO HEART: A CALL TO ACTION

♥   If you fit any of the three categories above, know someone who
does, or want to prevent being caught in a *heart marriage* in the future,
find a comfortable place and read this book, *My Heart Got Married And
I Didn't Know It.*

2

How to Recognize the Signs

Do You Have a Heart Marriage?

DEBBIE AND MIKE

DEBBIE AND MIKE LIVED in Baltimore, Maryland, and started dat-ing as high school seniors. Debbie didn't really like school and was an average student. Mike was not interested in academics but excelled in every art class he took. They smoked marijuana infrequently on the weekends. They had both had several casual sexual relationships before they met and were having sex by their third official date. After high school graduation, Debbie studied to be a dental hygienist and continued to live at home. Mike was a freelance photographer and moved into an apart-ment. Debbie began to spend many nights with Mike, usually lying to her parents that she was staying with a friend. She decided to move out of her parent's house into an apartment with a girlfriend, mostly so she could spend more time with Mike without having to continue to deceive her parents about her whereabouts. Mike eventually moved his belongings in with Debbie and her roommate because his work was unpredictable and he didn't have adequate finances to maintain his own place. The room-mate moved out after six months leaving Debbie and Mike living together by default.

Neither set of parents approved of their living arrangements, and Debbie's parents were not supportive of a marriage since Mike was not regularly employed. Mike did not feel he was ready to settle down al-though he did love Debbie. Debbie attempted to break off the relationship several times, even consulting a therapist at one point. They had a volatile relationship, but Mike blamed their fights on his artistic temperament, and would always cajole his way back into Debbie's life via the bed. They lived together tumultuously for five years and then finally married one afternoon in a low-key ceremony in a local judge's chamber. None of their family or friends attended. Six months later, Debbie moved out and into her own apartment. They tried to reconcile several times, but it was clear the marriage was not going to work. Their divorce was final a year later. The hurt and pain was so great that neither of them has married again, and Debbie has been in counseling for the past twenty years.

Mike and Debbie show all four of the classic signs of *heart marriage*—sexual intimacy, cohabitation, monogamy, and reluctance to marry over time. Quite possibly the heartache they experienced that has shadowed their lives could have been avoided if they had understood *heart marriage* and the risks involved.

DO YOU HAVE A HEART MARRIAGE?

There are four major indicators in determining whether a relationship has shifted from serious boy/girlfriend status into that of *heart marriage*. Recognizing at least three of these behaviors in a relationship may indicate *heart marriage*. Every relationship is different, but there are some fairly easy behaviors to evaluate.

Sign 1: Sexual Intimacy

In the current culture, it is very common for dating couples to become sexually intimate quickly. The biology of the sex drive makes it very powerful, and with easily available birth control and a movement away from strict religious and moral codes, many people feel that sex is a purely physical activity or tension reliever. While it is true that many people engage in one night stands or casual sex with many partners, that is not what we are talking about here. The sexual intimacy that leads to *heart marriage* comes from two people who like or love each other and are regularly having sexual relations. The sexual intimacy doesn't have to be immediate intercourse. It can be oral sex early in the relationship or mutual masturbation that quickly moves into sexual intercourse. One difficulty with early sexual involvement in a relationship is that the sex takes precedence over other shared activities and can therefore limit a couple from truly knowing each other. Sex and the bond it creates can act as a reconciler of differences and in mature relationships that can be positive. However, when sex is engaged in prematurely in a relationship, before couples know one another well, it can mask differences that would have shown the pairing to be unsustainable for the long term.

Even in this post-sexual revolution era, modern culture still occasionally gives a nod toward the idea that sexual relationships by their very nature are not casual or insignificant. In the popular movie *Vanilla Sky,* the Tom Cruise character has a sexual relationship with a woman played by Cameron Diaz. She struggles to handle their breakup and in her confrontation of him says, "Don't you know that when you sleep with someone, your body makes a promise whether you do or not?" (*Vanilla Sky*, directed by Cameron Crowe, 2001). The words of this character reflect very well an aspect of the bond that takes place within a sexual relationship.

There are emotional and physiological components to the intimacy of regular sexual activity that does bind hearts together. Sex inherently exposes one's vulnerability just by the act of being naked. There is also some recognition that a pregnancy can result, even if birth control is being used. So there is a level of trust, even if unspoken, in an ongoing sexual relationship that a pregnancy will become a shared responsibility. There is also a physiologic component to the intimacy of regular sexual relations with the surge of oxytocin in both males and females during sex and orgasm. Oxytocin is a hormone and neurotransmitter that is nicknamed "the bonding hormone" and "the love hormone" because of its binding properties. It provides a sense of calm and well-being and creates a desire for further contact with the individuals inciting its release. (Gutierrez and Stimmel, "Management," 823–831)

Debbie and Mike are a good example of *heart marriage* with the sexual intimacy indicator. While they had experienced casual sexual activity with other partners before they met, they quickly began to have regular sex with each other early in the relationship. They did not believe that a sexual relationship was anything more than good fun between consenting adults. For a time, Mike was able to use the emotional connection that sex provided as a way to keep Debbie from leaving him. They did not realize that over time their sexual relationship had bonded them together much like husband and wife.

Sign 2: Monogamy

The couples whose hearts have married practice monogamy. They feel they are in a serious relationship and are not seeking other partners. They cannot imagine a life with anyone else. They may even state to friends and family that they will be with this person forever and they do not expect to have another partner. However, often this is not being said to each other. There is a "forever but never" feeling—they think they will be together forever, but they never commit formally to a future.

Being able to maintain a monogamous relationship over time is a positive occurrence because it demonstrates fidelity and some level of maturity. Friends and family may say, "You have dated for ten years, but have not married; let me fix you up with my friend, cousin, etc." When the heart is married, couples usually avoid any new romantic possibilities. Since they are heart married, dating someone else feels to them like marital infidelity. Monogamy is a behavior that mimics an expectation in true legal marriage. The problem here is that both partners miss opportunities that could result in fuller relationships and real marriage.

Mike and Debbie were also monogamous during their seven-plus years together. Mike would tease Debbie about other women, but he never pursued another sexual relationship while they were together. Debbie fantasized about a more ideal life partner, but in many ways felt she deserved Mike. Practicing monogamy, in conjunction with other *heart marriage* signs, may indicate the occurrence of *heart marriage*.

Sign 3: Cohabiting

Couples who live together in a romantic partnership and share expenses, meals, and housework are at risk for falling into *heart marriage*. Intimacy inevitably develops as a result of sharing a life together. Not having the commitment to safeguard this intimacy can be disastrous as couples erect walls to protect themselves. The logistical difficulty of separating, once a couple lives together, becomes a false and unhelpful reason to stay together.

Couples who cohabit can be very deliberate about the arrangement or they can evolve into living together. Evolving into cohabitation usually happens when both persons have their own places but increasingly spend time in one of the homes. The couple may never completely move in together, but for all practical purposes they are cohabiting. Either way, if you ask a cohabiting couple, "Why don't you get married since you are already living as husband and wife?" they usually respond, "We are not ready to get married." For whatever reason, they do not feel ready to take that formal step into matrimony. Unfortunately, they are often already heart married. When the reasons they are not ready to marry surface, the cohabiting couple realizes they are not ready because this person is not the right one for them.

Mike and Debbie's cohabitation evolved over time. Mike moved in with Debbie and her roommate due to a financial crunch. They progressed further into living together when Debbie's roommate moved out. For all practical purposes, they were living as husband and wife, but were not ready to be husband and wife.

Sign 4: Reluctance to Marry Over Time

Couples who have been together for a long time but have not legally married may already have a *heart marriage*. Early on, they may assume or hope they will marry, but as time goes on, one or both parties may feel reluctant to marry, even though they know that friends and family are beginning to expect it. These couples may even say, "Why do we need to get married? We're already like a married couple without the license." At the core, though they may not verbally acknowledge it, they may recognize that their relationship has serious defects that would not weather a formal commitment. So, they continue to delay marriage and stay together under the false illusion that it will be easier to break up if they are not legally married.

Quite frequently, however, one member of the couple will finally pressure the other to marry with words that sound something like, "We either need to get married or break up." This is a dangerous ultimatum, as these feelings are the polar opposite of one another. When this feeling arises in a relationship, it probably is time to break up or get a *heart divorce*.

In the case of Mike and Debbie, they eventually decided to marry, rather spontaneously, and hoped it would improve the relationship. They didn't even tell their families until after the marriage had happened. This is a classic reaction to the presence of *heart marriage*. The couple realizes that the relationship is not right, but doesn't know what to do about it. They hope that legal marriage will fix their problems. This couple may have been able to separate without resorting to legal marriage and divorce had they understood what was happening in their relationship.

Remember, all relationships are different, but if sexual intimacy, monogamy, cohabiting, and reluctance to marry over time are a part of your relationship, it is very possible that you are heart married. In the next chapters, we will look at how each factor binds a couple together just as if they had said, "I do."

Taking It to Heart: A Call to Action

❤ Look back at the quiz you took at the end of chapter 1. Think about your answers in light of the signs that describe *heart marriage*. Now ask yourself directly, "Am I heart married or in danger of falling into a *heart marriage*?" Whatever your answer, keep reading!

❤ When you read about the signs of *heart marriage*, did the relationship of a friend or relative come to mind? If so, give them a copy of the book so they can understand clearly what is going on and how they can improve the situation.

3

Sexual Intimacy—The Great Deceiver

The Role Sexual Intimacy Plays in Marrying the Heart

A LMOST WITHOUT EXCEPTION, WHERE there is regular sexual intimacy between a couple there is *heart marriage.* Even in today's society
with its loosened moral values and fewer religious mandates, sexual intimacy is still associated by many with love and marriage. To some extent,
families teach it and churches preach it. Schools often have family life
curricula that promote abstinence as the healthiest single lifestyle, even
as they inform students of responsible protection measures for unwanted
pregnancies and sexually transmitted diseases. Meanwhile, the media
sends hypersexualized messages to viewers promoting casual, inconse-
quential sex in everything from daytime drama to primetime sitcoms.

Young people are as conflicted as society in their views of abstinence
and sexuality. A growing number of them are not practicing abstinence
while simultaneously delaying marriage, resulting in more couples routinely involved in sexually intimate relationships outside of marriage. The
problem is that those same couples may not realize that regular sexual activity with a person for whom they feel love or affection, binds the couple
together and, in effect, marries their hearts. Once that happens, it is more
difficult and painful to sever the relationship even when it is warranted.
When sexual intimacy is an integral part of a relationship, the couple is
often deceived into thinking that marriage is the predictable and only
logical next step for them. If there is unrest or stress in the relationship,
they may even blame it on the fact that they aren't married and believe

that their relationship will improve when they say "I do." Or, on the other hand, if they experience doubts, they may tell themselves that they are free to separate whenever they like, yet, when they try, the separation is too painful or feels too emotionally risky.

WHY IS SEXUAL INTIMACY SO POWERFUL AND DECEIVING?

The very nature of sexual intercourse is that it is literally a physical joining of two people. The couple is physically connected and become one being for a time of intense pleasure. The practical purpose of sexual intimacy at its most basic level is to create another human being who is a part of each of the individuals involved. This miraculous happening is one of the closest physical connections that humans can have; and therefore, is accompanied by intense emotions—passion, feelings of warmth and closeness, a sense of satisfaction and peace, and, at its best, love. This physical connecting is powerful and over time can marry the heart.

There is a physiologic hormonal component to the bonding that accompanies sexual intercourse and other sexual behaviors such as oral sex, intense petting, or masturbation. Oxytocin has been called the "hormone of love" or the "bonding hormone" for its ability to induce feelings of love, altruism, warmth, tenderness, togetherness, bonding, and satisfaction during bodily contact. (Margolis, *O: The Intimate*, par. 4–5) The hormone oxytocin is present in both males and females. Oxytocin has long been known to play an important role in the facilitation of childbirth and breastfeeding. It has now been shown that blood levels of oxytocin spike during orgasm for men and women. Oxytocin blood levels also rise with touch. The effects of oxytocin are magnified for women due to the higher levels of estrogen, a female hormone. Estrogen enhances the action of oxytocin. The release of oxytocin during orgasm and sexual activity is a primal response and compels the couple involved to continue the relationship. This is a strong biological element that happens in relationships that are sexual. (Margolis, par. 4–5) The bonding action of oxytocin plays a role in the development of *heart marriage*.

Emotionally and psychologically, there are basically three different underlying paths leading to *heart marriage* that originate from sexual intimacy. The first of these may be *seeking absolution from guilt*. Many young women and men are taught in this society that sex is wrong and sinful outside of marriage. These are powerful messages and can success-fully prevent young people from engaging in premarital sex. Too often, however, as young people grow up, fall in love, and face the raging emo-tions and desires associated with that love; they become involved sexually anyway. Since they have been taught that this is a wrong choice, guilt feel-ings ensue. The only way to make the guilt go away, other than to stop the sexual behavior, is to be married. Thus, even if this doesn't happen con-cretely, it happens in the heart. The couple is heart married. They become monogamous, feel like a part of each other's lives, consult each other on decisions, no longer consider themselves to be single, and fully anticipate making the union official at some appropriate time in the future.

The second path is that of *seeking congruence between behavior and values*. As young people mature and come to their own conclusions, they may not dwell on sexual intimacy outside of marriage as wrong or sinful. Instead they see sex as special and a part of loving someone. They respect themselves and want a special relationship with their partner, one that is different from all others. This mindset leads people to the notion that they will become intimate only if they are in love. The difficulty with this is that many relationships feel like love in the beginning. Both individuals are so totally focused on each other and shower each other with loving behavior that it feels like love. Sometimes it is. Other times, however, it may simply be the honeymoon stage of a relationship that is subject to grow cold if there is only the physical attraction to keep it going. Once a couple is sexually intimate, in order to maintain congruence between their values and behavior, the couple may tend to idealize the relationship, making it better than it is and convincing themselves that they are in love. After becoming sexually intimate out of feelings of love and devotion, *heart marriage* may occur. The intentionality and commitment of legal mar-riage is missing, but the heart and physical connection is strong. When a couple is heart married, they feel that they can't just walk away from each other and if they do break up, they immediately miss the closeness and want the person back.

The final path that sexual intimacy follows on the way to the heart is that of *mistaking sexual closeness for love*. Love, acceptance, and belong-ing are higher order needs of humans and often the connection between individuals through sexual intimacy is so powerful that it brings with it those feelings. This feeling is no doubt related to the effects of oxytocin that is secreted in high levels during sex, orgasm, and touching. At no other time has the couple felt so close to anyone as when they are sexually intimate. These feelings are mistaken for love and the heart gets married. Love, unlike sexual intimacy alone, is the ongoing decision to act in the best interest of another individual and the ability to put another person's well being first. While love and a loving relationship are enriched through sexual intimacy, love is not sexual intimacy alone.

Mistaking sexual intimacy for love is more likely when a relationship becomes sexual very quickly. No matter how liberated society has become, sex is an intense experience that often masks as love. It makes a person feel good and close and cared for, but it can be very deceptive. After the fact, individuals may label their emotions as lust rather than love, but at the time, it is exciting and romantic and truly feels unlike anything else. Unfortunately, when a relationship becomes sexual in its early stages, the bonding that takes place is often primarily sexual even if one or the other in the relationship feels love. This may explain why so many unhealthy relationships hang together for so long based on very little other than sex. There is a danger with hasty sexual intimacy if one ultimately wants a lasting relationship. In a world where people are seeking love and closeness, and in a culture where impatience is common, the sexual bond is not only intense but is immediate. It takes time to develop a truly loving relationship that is built on mutual respect. As we look at the concept of *heart marriage*, we would suggest that the intertwining of couples through sexual intimacy is complex and takes different turns for different people, however, to some degree, mistaking sex for love is consistent throughout all of the examples of *heart marriage*.

BRIANA AND DAVID

Briana was an exceptional young teenager—smart, pretty, popular, and very involved in church and school activities. She was mature for her age and wanted to have a boyfriend. Briana set high standards for herself and had academic goals to go to college and become a writer and college professor. But she always knew that her most cherished dream was to be married and have children.

Briana loved her parents and was particularly intent on not disappointing them. Her family was religious, attending church every time the doors opened. The doctrine was strict. She heard many sermons about the dangers of drinking, smoking, and premarital sex. Lust was a sin, sex was to be reserved for marriage, and a truly good Christian would only have one sexual partner. Sins could be forgiven, but lost virginity could not be regained. In her personal life, she had goals also, vowing to herself that she would not drink or smoke and would only have sex with her husband.

One summer, early in high school, Briana met David, an older guy who attended college in a neighboring town. He was handsome and funny, and she was flattered when he flirted with her and asked her for a date. As she got to know him, she was excited because he had been brought up in a strong Christian environment and had the same beliefs as she did. Even though he was considerably older, she felt safe, because he would surely respect her desire not to have sex.

That was not to be, and fairly predictably this high school girl and college boy's relationship quickly became sexual. Briana repeatedly vowed to stop. David would agree initially, but their sexual activity continued. Because of Briana's conflicting feelings about premarital sex, they pretty quickly stopped having intercourse. They continued, however, to pet heavily and participate in other sexually intimate behavior. The couple broke up once in high school for a very brief period of time. Briana was devastated even though her gut told her it was best. After a week David came back professing his love; she gave in; and they resumed the relationship, thinking that it must be the right thing to do.

Briana finished high school and attended the same college as David. They fought often—usually over little things. He was jealous and didn't want her to speak to other guys. He didn't like her friends and wanted to spend his time on the weekends playing golf, hunting, or fishing. Briana seriously considered dating other people and was often asked out, but she couldn't bring herself to be unfaithful to David and always said no. When asked, her explanation was that she knew she and David would eventually get married, so why date anyone else. It seemed senseless.

When David asked Briana to marry him, she had some nagging concerns, but to avoid any more temptation, she decided to go ahead. After all, they had now dated four years; he had a good job and she thought it would get better when they married. It didn't and Briana soon was miserable. David became more and more controlling and jealous. He put her down and made fun of the things that interested her. They had some good times and a nice circle of friends, but he spent many weekends involved in his own sporting activities regardless of what Briana wanted to do. He reminded her that she knew this about him before they married and, in fact, she did. She decided to go to graduate school and though David agreed, he resented the time she spent studying. They seemed to disagree on everything. They became more and more estranged, except when they had sex.

David remained faithful, but after so many accusations, Briana became involved with another man. Knowing that was wrong, she quickly broke off the relationship, but finally knew without a doubt that she should never have married David. Briana came to realize that their sexual intimacy had caused her heart to marry David. The ceremony really just legitimized the relationship. She had to make it official with a wedding and a wedding ring. She felt guilty that she had sex with David and thought the only way to "make it right" was to get married. They did feel love for each other, but David was the wrong person for Briana and she was the wrong person for him. When they met, she was too young to really know herself or what she wanted. David didn't know how to deal with her strong will and intellectual curiosity, so he just tried to control her. It took one separation and several years, but finally Briana filed for divorce after a four-year courtship and a six-year marriage.

This is just one example of how sexual intimacy can cause the heart to marry and actually deceive the couple into believing that they are meant for each other. This couple had strong religious beliefs around abstinence, and felt that their sexual involvement meant that they were married in God's eyes. Regularly occurring sexual intimacy between two individuals does bind them together. It makes them feel so intertwined that it is very painful when they try to break up. Often the female, particularly, will begin to feel the need to formalize this long-term sexual relationship. Even if legal marriage is not on the horizon for one reason or another, the couple becomes heart married without realizing it.

Additionally, there are times when the head tells one or both partners that there is something wrong, but when the couple tries to break up, they crave the closeness they have had sexually. Often everything in the relationship seems wrong, but when they come together sexually, they feel close and are deceived into believing that it is love. The problem is that sexual closeness alone is not love and can't take the place of a loving, respectful, and reciprocal relationship. In many ways, sexual intimacy can be the absolute worst thing for a relationship because it causes a false sense of closeness that prevents the couple from rationally assessing their compatibility and feelings for each other.

Before leaving this subject, we would like to introduce you to Marcia and Joe whose decision to be sexually intimate resulted in their hanging onto a bad relationship for years. In this case, however, rather than guilt, it was the natural tendency to seek congruence between their values and their sexual behavior that married their hearts.

MARCIA AND JOE

Marcia and Joe were responsible, clear thinking college seniors. They had almost completed their educations and were focused on careers. Both had solid backgrounds, good families, and were taught the importance of integrity. They looked at life's issues practically, but also wanted to make a contribution to society. Both Marcia and Joe believed that sex should be accompanied by love. They felt strongly that there was more to love than sex and recognized that sex can be deceiving in regard to feelings. Each decided individually that they would not participate in casual sex. They believed sex should be special and reserved for serious relationships. They felt it was more important to focus on developing a friendship before moving into a sexually intimate relationship.

For the most part, their behavior had been congruent with these beliefs. Marcia did have a sexual relationship early in college that she thought was serious. The breakup was very painful for her and she became even more resolved to delay future sexual intimacy until she knew that both she and any future boyfriend were equally in love and committed.

Joe also was committed to wait for the right girl, for both practical and romantic reasons. He disapproved of all of the war stories about sex that his fraternity brothers shared and didn't feel comfortable talking about sexual encounters as conquests. By the time he was a senior, he had been involved sexually a couple of times, but it just didn't feel right. He didn't beat himself up about it, but realized he had a more idealistic view of sex and was not interested in casual encounters.

Marcia and Joe seemed perfect for each other. When they met in an upper division business class they hit it off right away. They started dating and discussed everything, including their views about sex. When after six months they believed they were in love, they began a sexual relationship. By the end of the year, they were spending most weekends together in Joe's apartment. Marcia couldn't imagine being with anyone else. She had met the man she would marry, although they had much to accomplish and neither wanted to rush.

After she graduated, Marcia started a dual program to obtain her Master's in Business Administration and a law degree and Joe took a job in his field and began to work on his career. The two kept separate apartments but spent most of their time together. Their sexual relationship continued to be good, and they settled into a very comfortable relationship, talking about the future in general terms.

During Marcia's second year in grad school, the relationship began to change subtly at first and then more drastically. Joe became more focused on work and revealed that he intended to return to his hometown, where he would learn the family business and take over when his dad retired. It was a lucrative business, but the town was a small, close-knit place and Marcia felt like an outsider. She liked theatre, museums, and the amenities of a large city, but Joe assured her they could enjoy all those things by visiting the large city nearby. It bothered Marcia that it took Joe so long to share this lifelong dream with her, but she pushed it out of her mind. When they had talked about the future and that her best career choice was to join a large firm with a business law practice, he was agreeable. He said he could pursue his business career anywhere. He mentioned that he might ultimately go into the family business but that it would be ten or fifteen years before he would consider it.

Gradually, Marcia noticed that Joe's responses to things they had discussed began to change. The changes were slight, but made a difference. For instance, they wanted children and Marcia believed in putting resources into private school. Joe originally voiced agreement, but now began to say that the public school in his hometown was good enough for him and should be good enough for his children. It bothered Marcia that Joe was reversing the things they once agreed upon. She sensed that he was not as truthful and trustworthy as she thought, and often said what he believed people wanted to hear. She noticed he turned conversations to himself and had little interest in her career. In response to her criticism, he said it was she who was self-absorbed and that she should be willing to adjust to his goals.

Marcia wondered whether Joe was committed to forging a future that would be good for both of them, but whenever they had a disagreement, Joe would do something romantic and they would end up making love and making up. This scared her, because she had committed herself to the relationship. She loved Joe and felt that he truly loved her. She knew that Joe had many good points and began to doubt herself; wondering if she were too picky and selfish, like Joe told her. After all, they couldn't stay mad at each other and sex was a big part of that. It seemed that no matter what else was wrong, when they were together physically, it felt like they were meant for each other.

The situation changed when Marcia was studying for final exams and interviewing with law firms in several cities. To her surprise, Joe appeared one night to tell her he didn't think their relationship would work. He said he loved her, but knew she would never be happy in his hometown and that he couldn't disappoint his father. He said he was very sorry, but that he had been realizing this for quite some time. They both cried and she begged him to go to counseling, pleading that they had committed them-selves to each other. Joe refused and insisted that it was best to break it off. Marcia somehow got through her exams. Joe moved to his hometown within the month and their four-year relationship ended. Two years later, Marcia was still struggling. She started her law career and dated some, but ran into trouble when the relationships moved toward sexual intimacy. She still had the same value system, but it was more and more difficult to avoid having sex. She didn't want to go there again, sensing that the sex had kept her emotionally bound to Joe. She entered counseling in order to move forward.

Although Marcia and Joe did not make it to the altar, they wasted years in a *heart marriage*. In counseling, Marcia realized that she too had begun to have doubts about her relationship with Joe, and probably should have broken it off herself. Her value system clearly viewed love as a prerequisite for sexual intimacy and identified sexual intimacy with marriage. This forced her to continue to idealize her relationship with Joe and view it as better than it really was. Marcia and Joe had all the signs of *heart marriage* except cohabitation.

Marcia was able to finally see that their sexual intimacy was the most binding aspect of their relationship. Both had made a decision against casual sex and their values indicated that they felt sexual intimacy should be a result of love. Although they didn't openly admit that marriage was a necessity, they clearly felt that their sexual intimacy was a sign that the relationship was real, that it was serious, and that it would most likely lead to marriage. As it turned out, Marcia was much more bound to Joe than he to her, and her heart, without question, had gotten married. Although she didn't carry strong guilt feelings around their intimacy, in order for her behavior to be congruent with her values, she had to hold onto the idea that she was in love with Joe. Being heart married, she convinced herself that her misgivings were frivolous and not worthy of a breakup. It was only after counseling that Marcia realized that she had become heart married and had, in effect, gone through the same pain of a divorce, even though it had been a *heart divorce*. With help, she looked closely at her values and her behavior and began to understand how her choices had created a situation where she allowed herself to be deceived about the relationship. Knowing this, she was able to accept the situation, work through her pain, and move forward with her life. She became more secure in her ability to make good choices in future relationships.

In summary, sexual intimacy played a critical role in marrying the hearts of both Marcia and Joe and Briana and David. Although Marcia and Joe did not have the strong religious beliefs held by Briana and David or feel the same level of guilt, they clearly associated sexual intimacy with marriage. Even with today's changing attitudes toward sex, many young men and women still grow up making that same connection. Moreover, it is sexual intimacy that sets the marital relationship apart from all other relationships between men and women, so it is no wonder that regular sexually intimacy between two people binds the heart and creates *heart marriage*.

Because we have been created as sexual beings with sexual desires, the longer marriage is delayed, the more likely today's couples will engage in sexual intimacy. While today's young people may see the need to delay marriage, they often do not see the need to delay sex. As a result, they become sexually involved fairly early in a relationship. This can be very dangerous when such intimacy occurs before couples really know and understand each other and have time to determine whether or not they have the same hopes, aspirations, and views of what marriage is and what they want for their future. When sexual intimacy occurs early, it becomes increasingly difficult to use good sound judgment to make decisions of the heart.

This chapter has examined sexual intimacy as a key sign of *heart marriage*. Usually, sexual intimacy happens first, followed by monogamy, but these two signs can be reversed in order of occurrence. A couple may start a monogamous relationship and then become sexually involved. The next chapter will look at monogamy as an indicator of *heart marriage*, but before reading on, consider the Call to Action below.

Taking It to Heart: A Call to Action

❤   Imagine your relationship without sex. Draw a line down the center of a piece of paper. On one side, write all of the ways that you and your partner are compatible. On the other side, write the areas where you feel you are incompatible or have significant differences. Consider which side is more compelling. Be honest with yourself.

❤   Now think about your present relationship and when you feel the closest to your partner. If the answer is when you are having sex, make the decision to eliminate it from your relationship for a month. Be honest with your partner about it. Tell him/her you want to be sure you can enjoy each other without physical intimacy. At the end of the month answer this question again. When do you feel closest to your boy/girlfriend?

4

Monogamy

The Second Sign of Heart Marriage

T HE SECOND SIGN THAT indicates *heart marriage* has occurred is that the couple has embraced monogamy. Remember, *heart marriage* is a relationship in which the couple is intimately bound together and in which they practice the behaviors of marriage without the intentional and articulated agreement of both parties to be married. Monogamy is the practice of having a single sexual partner during a period of time. It has also been described as the state or custom of being married to one person at a time or of having one mate at a time. (Merriam-Webster's, "monogamy," lines 7–9) Clearly, there is a stated expectation of monogamy when a legal marriage has taken place.

Since the colonization of America, monogamy has been encouraged through laws and customs. In the United States, Europe, and much of the world, it has been believed that legally corroborated monogamy benefits society by providing a safe union for sexual expression and by supplying predictable care and support for young and dependent children. These laws originated in large part from Judeo-Christian doctrine. If the expectation of monogamy is violated by infidelity, that infidelity provides a legal cause or grounds for divorce.

When monogamy is practiced in a romantic, sexually intimate relationship, it can be one indicator that *heart marriage* has taken place. Interestingly, while *heart marriage* occurs without spoken intent, monogamy in the relationship is usually verbally identified as an expectation. When a couple practices monogamy, they are indicating by their exclusive attention to each other that the relationship has value and is respected. The practice of monogamy indicates that the relationship is more than a friendship and that it has become special. It appears that in our modern culture there is a desire for the closeness, trust, and support that comes with such a special relationship.

The four indicators of *heart marriage* should not be considered as either good or bad, rather they are simply identifying markers to help couples understand where they are in their long term romantic relationships. There are positive and negative aspects of the *heart marriage* indicators of sexual intimacy, cohabitation, and reluctance to marry over time. However, the presence of monogamy as an indicator is a strongly positive characteristic of the relationship. The compromises and work involved with being in relationship require some level of maturity and commitment. When a couple is able to be faithful, sexually and emotionally, it is a valuable cornerstone to the partnership.

Monogamy adds value to a relationship in many ways, making it a desirable practice. One advantage of monogamy is increased protection from sexually transmitted diseases. A consequence of the sexual freedom in the post-sexual revolution has been the spread of sexually transmitted diseases like HIV/AIDS, genital herpes, chlamydia, hepatitis B, and several other highly communicable diseases. The United States has the highest rates of sexually transmitted diseases with estimates of 19 million new cases identified every year. (Centers for Disease Control, "Sexually Transmitted," lines 1–2) These diseases often have long term consequences, ranging from infertility and the potential to be harmful or fatal to the babies of infected mothers, to the death of the mother from liver failure or cancer. If a disease-free couple is monogamous, they do not risk exposure to sexually transmitted disease.

A monogamous relationship also insures that should pregnancy result, the parentage is known. This is comforting to most individuals and usually helps to insure that the conceived child will have support and nurture. There is some level of trust, even if unspoken, that the couple would handle a pregnancy together. This unspoken assumption can be dangerous because often when faced with the situation, the individuals have quite different ideas about how to deal with a pregnancy.

A monogamous sexual relationship also fosters a level of mutual trust that is difficult to establish and maintain when there is more than one partner. The exclusivity of monogamy allows the couple to relax and feel more at ease with each other. It decreases stress and uncertainty and unless there is a breach of fidelity, monogamy can free the couple of petty jealousy. Absent the stress of trying to impress or win the love of one's partner, the couple settles into a relationship that can grow and develop through spending time together, learning more about each other, and understanding each other's needs and relationship goals.

Since marriage laws explicitly name monogamy as an expectation in the marriage contract, a monogamous dating relationship clearly imitates a facet of legal marriage. Although in isolation monogamy does not necessarily result in *heart marriage*, it is no wonder that when practiced along with sexual intimacy and cohabitation, often the heart feels a strong connection and binding together that is similar to legal marriage. This is especially the case if the relationship extends over a prolonged period of time. Quietly, *heart marriage* occurs and the couple is not even aware of it.

The main negative aspect of monogamy in *heart marriage* is that the *heart marriage* may have occurred even though the relationship is unhealthy or the couple is ill suited for each other. In this case, the practice of monogamy may result in missed opportunities for the couple to meet someone who would be a better match for a long-term sustained relationship. Not only are heart married couples not looking for other partners, they consciously reject the notion of exploring other relationships and avoid situations conducive to meeting people of the opposite sex. Since, by definition, the heart married couple has not openly discussed their future commitment to the relationship, time continues to pass by. For the woman, this has bigger consequences than for the man, if she wants to experience pregnancy and childbirth as a part of having a family. Fertility rates for women begin to drop after age twenty-seven and dramatically drop after age thirty-five. The decline in fertility rates for men is much slower and later (Hall, "Study Speeds," sec. A).

There are a couple of salient points to consider as to the why and how couples embrace the practice of monogamy. It is perhaps most common that a couple begins to date, casually at first, and as some time passes they realize that a special friendship is developing and that they enjoy each other's company. One indication of whether there is real interest in each other is whether or not the individuals have ceased to flirt with or date other people. In those heady first weeks of a new relationship, the participants may wonder, "Does he/she consider me as his/her boy/girlfriend yet?" At some point, this question may be asked directly, "Will you be my girl/boyfriend?" If the answer is yes, the couple will then clarify that they are now dating each other exclusively. After this agreement and declaration, the couple's relationship might become sexual. This seems to be the most logical progression and the pattern that has been practiced most often. Historically, if a couple became sexually involved, it was after being openly exclusive and monogamous.

Monogamy may also be established after the relationship has become sexual. This couple may date casually but become sexually involved before identifying themselves as an exclusive couple. This early sexual involvement happens for a number of reasons. The individuals may feel sex is just a physical expression of attraction that routinely accompanies dating and that exclusivity is not necessary. Often, dating and alcohol consumption go hand in hand. Alcohol tends to lower inhibitions and individuals may consent to sexual activity from which they normally would have refrained had they not been drinking. In some cases, one or both of the individuals may use sex as a way to hold the interest of the other or they may not want to appear to be prudish or outdated in their beliefs about sexuality. However it happens, the casually dating couple has sex and then they may seek to define the relationship as monogamous. It may be an unspoken assumption on the part of one or both of the participants. The couple will often embrace monogamy in order to establish it as a more serious relationship. This is particularly true when either of the individuals holds the value that sexual intimacy is associated with love or at least deep affection. This mindset is in keeping with the idea mentioned in chapter 3 that individuals tend to seek congruence between their values and their behavior.

All of the couples we have discussed thus far have practiced monogamy. Alice and James became monogamous shortly after they started dating their freshman year in college and were together exclusively for eight years before they married. Although James occasionally fantasized about other women, he remained faithful to Alice. Debbie and Mike were having sex by their third date, long before they could really have established a serious relationship, and they remained monogamous for five years prior to marrying. They had a stormy relationship and broke up a number of times, but these breakups did not involve dating anyone else. They quickly would miss each other, console themselves with sex, and resume their monogamous relationship. Marcia and Joe were monogamous for five years; right up until the day Joe delivered the "bombshell" that he did not think their relationship could work for the long haul. By that time, Marcia was finishing law school and was ready to settle down and marry. She was devastated. Even though she had some doubts about the relationship herself, she had remained faithful. She had "put all her eggs in one basket" and felt a great deal of resentment and pain for years to come. In the case of Briana and David, Briana's infidelity didn't occur until after they married and it was her way out of the marriage. Although they had been monogamous and faithful for four years of dating, in her mind, the marital cheating provided a clear violation of the legal marriage contract and thus she could rightly terminate the marriage.

It is not uncommon to see heart married couples experience infidelity although they have been monogamous for quite some time and continue to define their relationship as exclusive. This break with monogamy is seen as "cheating" even though the couple is not yet married, and often occurs as a way to end the relationship, even if it is an unconscious attempt. Unfortunately, instead of recognizing the cheating as a sign that a *heart divorce* is needed, the couple may get back together, rationalizing that "if we were married" this would not have happened. They proceed to the altar quickly and find that a legal marriage was not the solution either. However, as a married couple, they can then officially separate with a legal divorce and try to rebuild their lives.

In summary, the trust that develops in a sexually monogamous relationship is deeply binding. Monogamy, in conjunction with sexual intimacy, contributes to marriage of the heart. Monogamy promotes a comfort level in a relationship that can cause a couple to settle into a "marriage like" existence. While monogamy may add value to a relationship in a number of ways and can be an indication of a mature and committed relationship, it can also stand in the way of individuals exploring new relationships, even when they have doubts and are feeling reluctant to make a commitment to their partner with solid plans for the future.

After considering both sexual intimacy and monogamy and the roles these two practices play in a marriage of the heart, there are two remaining indicators, cohabitation and reluctance to marry over time. In the next chapter, we will look more closely at the practice of cohabitation, its prevalence in today's culture, and how it contributes to *heart marriage*.

Taking It to Heart: A Call to Action

❤ Think about your relationship in light of monogamy. Have both you and your partner verbalized that you are dating one another exclusively? Or are you assuming your partner is monogamous? Either way, if this aspect of your relationship has not been discussed, now is the time to do so.

❤ Consider if your relationship has had an episode (or more) of infidelity. If so, was it an attempt, subconsciously or overtly, to get out of the relationship? Did either of you justify, excuse, or defend the infidelity by saying, "Well, at least we aren't married" or, "It wouldn't have happened if we were married"? Now that you are gaining an understanding of *heart marriage*, you will want to reevaluate any episode of infidelity to determine why it happened. This requires that you give yourself some time to think about and reflect upon all facets of your relationship and how they work together.

5

Cohabitation

The Risky Business of Living Together

THE THIRD INDICATOR OF *heart marriage* is the practice of cohabitation. Living together may occur in several ways. Once a romantic relationship becomes sexually intimate, the couple begins to devote more time to one another. Soon they are spending nights together. At this point, it may simply make financial sense to split the rent and expenses on one place. The financial explanation is usually the articulated reason, while other reasons often remain unspoken. Another way cohabitation happens is in a more fluid arrangement where both participants keep their own living spaces. These couples are still spending most nights together, as well as meals and the other activities of daily life. However, they may say they are not living together because they maintain two residences. For all practical purposes, though, they are cohabiting. A final scenario is that many couples cohabit once they become engaged, have the date set, and are in the process of planning a wedding. Now referred to as prenuptial cohabitation, this practice is becoming more common in our culture. This scenario will not be discussed as an indicator of *heart marriage* since it only occurs once the intent to marry is agreed upon and plans are underway, unlike in the case of *heart marriage* where there is no clearly stated intention or plan to marry.

The number of couples living together before marriage has increased dramatically since 1960. (Alternatives to Marriage, par. 1) Although couples have lived together outside of marriage throughout the years, from a historical perspective, living together today is quite different from what could be seen prior to 1960. In the past, living together was often called common-law marriage. Common-law marriage still exists, but currently is only recognized and allowed in a few states—Alabama, Colorado, Iowa, Kansas, Montana, New Hampshire, Oklahoma, Rhode Island, South Carolina, Texas, Utah, and the District of Columbia. (*Wikipedia*, "common-law marriage," sec. 1, 7) For a relationship to have common-law marriage status in these states, the couple must cohabit for a specified number of years as well as present themselves as husband and wife to the community. The states that allow it may have other stipulations, but universally these couples must show intent and agreement to be married. They publicly declare themselves to be married. In years past, a community would often look upon these couples as married for the reason mentioned—they presented themselves as a married couple. Additionally, they often had children who resided with them and didn't really talk about the fact that they were not married.

The intentionality of the couple in a common-law arrangement is much different from the intent of couples who currently embrace cohabitation. Today's cohabiting couples clearly say they are living together and are not presenting themselves as married. They are usually presenting themselves as definitely not married. With this difference, come different emotional ramifications and risks. The remainder of the chapter will consider cohabitation as it most often occurs today. We will discuss some of the most common reasons that couples say they choose to cohabit as well as some of the risks involved.

There are many reasons given for this cultural shift in living arrangements. Numerous young people have suffered through the painful divorces of their parents and grandparents and are not eager to revisit that pain in their own adult relationships. While they are rightly responding in a protective mode, cohabiting will not necessarily prevent them from difficult relationships and breakups. They also view marriage as a highly valued ideal, but are purposely waiting until later to embrace it. The idea of marriage is so romanticized they fear that a successful marriage is an unattainable goal. So, in many ways, they settle for living together now and hope for a happy marriage later.

Young people are also hoping that age and maturity will give them an edge in the attainment of a healthy marriage. So they are living together now, waiting until they are older and wiser to try marriage. It is true that marriages after age twenty have a better chance of survival. Statistically,

70 percent of marriages before age twenty end in divorce, compared to around 40 percent of marriages failing when the marriage takes place after age twenty. (Collum, "Reality Check," par. 5–6). Maturity, however, is demonstrated in a wide spectrum of age groups and is more difficult to measure. It is a fallacy to think that age alone will increase the success of marriage, especially if destructive behaviors have been practiced in the ensuing years.

Since living together has lost much of its negative stigma, couples say that cohabitation seems like a viable option for trying out a relationship. It may be seen as a logical step in a relationship that is already sexual. Many are frightened by the odds of creating a successful marriage, since statistics show that around 40 percent of marriages end in divorce. Cohabiters may think that they will be less at risk emotionally if they live together and it doesn't work out than if they marry and then divorce.

One of the difficulties with living together is that many couples do not fully discuss their reasons for cohabiting. While a couple may openly discuss the financial savings of living together, they may also entertain unspoken reasons. Men and women often have different reasons for cohabiting. According to Pamela Stock, Associate Professor of Sociology at the University of Michigan, women will frequently see cohabitation as a step before marriage to that partner, while men see cohabitation as something that is done before making a commitment. (Jayson, "Cohabitation," sec. L) These two reasons are very different and set the couple up for hurt and disappointment later in the relationship. This is the perfect situation for *heart marriage* to occur for one or both of the people. When all the reasons to live together are not clearly articulated, openness and honesty become a challenge.

We see that some of the reasons given for living together then become the risks to the couple and the relationship. Risk means being exposed to the chance of injury or loss; risk can be dangerous or hazardous. The risk taken with living together in a romantic relationship is that a *heart marriage* can take place. Remember that a *heart marriage* is a relationship in which the couple is intimately bound together and in which they practice the behaviors of marriage without the intentional or articulated agreement to marry. It is risky to the emotional health of the parties involved when a *heart marriage* takes place. For example, if a woman sees cohabiting as a step toward marriage, she will be disappointed when a wedding does not soon become a reality. She may feel that somehow she has failed in the relationship since it has not resulted in a proposal and engagement or she may feel used and disrespected, even though there was never a promise of marriage.

Another risk is that of unintended pregnancy. While many birth control options are readily available, unplanned pregnancies do occur. A couple may be fastidious about avoiding pregnancy, but it can still happen. Cohabiting women and men may have very different ideas about how a pregnancy would be handled should it occur. If a couple has evolved into their living arrangement, they may never have discussed the possibility of unintended pregnancy. In the heat of early sexual involvement, birth control may be discussed and used but its possible failure is often not addressed. This scenario not only involves the couple, it brings another very vulnerable human being into the equation, one who will need nurturing, loving, and protecting for a minimum of twenty years.

There is also the risk that cohabiting will not increase the chance of later marital success and happiness. Studies reflect conflicting results about the success of marriage after cohabitation. Some clearly say that cohabiting before marriage does not affect the success of the marriage, indicating that cohabitation neither hurts nor helps. Other studies report that in terms of divorce and marital happiness, marriages that were preceded by cohabitation are less successful than those that were not. (DiCaro, "NFI Releases," 4–5) A more universally accepted finding, and one that has real implications for today's couples, is the evidence that serial cohabiters are at a higher risk of divorce once they marry. This is important because once a couple has lived together; there is the risk that it becomes a habitual pattern of behavior.

Finally, living together in a way that looks like marriage may bring about marriage of the heart. The daily sharing of life's intimate and mundane moments will bind two people together. Often the cohabiting couple makes joint purchases for the household and begins to establish traditions together. The familiarity of waking up together and going to bed together promotes a sense of oneness and the two feel emotionally invested in the home that they have created. The one thing individuals hope to avoid by living together is the emotional anguish of breaking up. But this is not to be. As more people live together, there is anecdotal evidence that these separations are as difficult as divorce. Because the concept of *heart marriage* has not been studied and understood, the pain that accompanies their attempts at breaking up catches the couple unaware.

JAY AND JACKIE

Jay and Jackie met as first year medical students at the University of Virginia. They noticed each other the first week of class and very cleverly arranged to be in the same study group. They enjoyed being together and quickly realized they had a common background. Both were Jewish, both were firstborn children, and both had hoped to become physicians since junior high school. Jay was from Florida, Jackie from New York. They spent most of their time together, both in the classroom and after class in study group. Although they felt an immediate sexual attraction, they resolved not to date due to the long road ahead for each of them to become physicians. When they returned to second semester classes that first year, their resolve crumbled and they became romantically involved. They initially discussed keeping their lives separate due to the long hours and the focus necessary for medical school. But by the end of second semester the two were spending most of their time in Jackie's apartment.

Jay kept his apartment through the second year of medical school, but then moved his things officially into Jackie's place since he had been living there anyway. Their parents embraced the relationship and thought living together was very practical and even encouraged it. Their relationship wasn't easy and the long hours at school and the hospital took a physical and mental toll. The sex was great. In many ways it was a physical outlet for the immense stress of medical school. Jay and Jackie often joked that if they should break up, they would still get together for sex. Both entertained flirtations with others, but never very seriously. They did notice that they avoided controversial subjects; neither of them wanted to fight. Increasingly, Jackie felt she was unable to voice her opinion about where they would go for residency. Jay assumed they would eventually marry, but did not feel the time was right. They married after medical school mostly so that they could apply to the residency "match program" as a couple and live in the same place.

Their respective medical residencies in pediatrics and vascular surgery were grueling. They increasingly felt isolated from one another and wondered if a baby would help bridge the growing estrangement. They quickly became pregnant and delivered a beautiful baby girl. During the baby's first year of life, Jay and Jackie realized they had very different ideas about childrearing and religion, even though they were both raised Jewish. They realized they had never discussed many of their innermost feelings and hopes for life outside of medical practice. They were divorced before the baby had her second birthday.

Jackie and Jay are a good example of *heart marriage* with all the telltale signs. They were living the stressful life of medical students and fell into living together because it seemed practical. Once they began to date, they were sexually intimate and monogamous. Initially, they did avoid moving in together, deciding to keep separate apartments, however, the more time Jay spent in Jackie's apartment, maintaining the two residences didn't seem reasonable. Once they were living together, however, they truly were "acting like a married couple." They were sharing the everyday activities, routines, and decisions that come with occupying the same living space, further binding them together without any articulated agreement for the future. While they didn't delay marriage for a long time, the marriage took place because it would help with their residency placement. Their hearts were married and they didn't have the time or energy to break up in the midst of preparing for the next stage of education. Unfortunately, Jackie and Jay married because it seemed like the thing to do. In their case, they even had a child to try to make sense of the relationship. Ultimately, the time and energy involved with the divorce forced Jackie to take a year off from residency to regain some emotional stability. Had Jackie and Jay been aware that their hearts would possibly marry if they lived together in a romantic relationship, they might have chosen another path that would have been less painful. Fortunately, both Jackie and Jay remarried successfully to other people.

The emotions of the heart are difficult to explain and have been discussed at length for eternity. In many ways, the passionate nature of the heart remains a mystery. Since there has been a cultural shift in the acceptance of living together and because many people are embracing cohabitation, there will have to be strategies to explore and address what the ramifications will be later in life. Even though living together is very common, marriage is still a valued and hoped-for occurrence for most people. The idea that cohabitation and *heart marriage* pose a risk to future healthy marriages needs to be more fully understood and discussed.

The final sign of a *heart marriage* is a reluctance to marry over time. The next chapter will explore how this inability to plan for the future can indicate that *heart marriage* has occurred. The reluctance to marry over time is referred to as the pivotal sign of a *heart marriage*, because it not only indicates that *heart marriage* has likely occurred, it also strongly signals that some change of course is warranted. Before you leave this chapter on cohabitation and move on to learn about this final sign, think about your present or past relationships and take this simple quiz to help you think more about your own living arrangements.

COHABITATION QUIZ: AM I COHABITING?

1. Are you and your romantic partner living in a shared space and sharing expenses for rent, groceries, etc?

    ❤ If yes, duh! You are indeed living together!

2. Do you and your romantic partner have different living spaces but spend three or four or even more nights together at one place?

    ❤ If yes, most likely, your heart thinks you are cohabiting even if your brain says you are not.

3. Do you and your partner maintain separate living spaces but spend occasional nights together, such as less than once a week?

    ❤ In this case, even if the answer is yes, you are maintaining some autonomy, and this would not be considered cohabiting.

Taking It to Heart: A Call to Action

❤ If you answered yes to the first two questions in the quiz, reflect back on how you and your partner began to live together. Did you discuss it first? Did you just sort of slide into it and then decide to let one of your living spaces go because it didn't make financial sense to pay for two places? How has it worked out?

❤ Discuss with your partner why you both decided to cohabit, remembering that often people have very different reasons for this. If one of you hoped the cohabitation would lead to marriage and the other one just wanted to try out the relationship, where are you now in that process?

6

Reluctance to Marry Over Time

The Pivotal Sign of Heart Marriage

THE FOURTH AND FINAL sign of *heart marriage* is the reluctance to marry over time. This is called the pivotal sign because it can be both a signal that the heart is married and simultaneously, an indication that *heart divorce* is likely needed. Reluctance to marry over time implies that the relationship is a prolonged one and the couple has usually been together for years rather than months. Reluctance to marry over time often catapults the couple into marriage when perhaps a *heart divorce* is more warranted. This may be the case particularly if one partner becomes impatient and presents an ultimatum to marry or break up, or if the couple just becomes weary with their conflicting feelings. However, in this chapter reluctance to marry over time will be discussed as a signal to the couple that, without intending it, the heart has married and the knot is tied.

Typically the most common reasons couples feel this reluctance to marry over time can be categorized in one of three ways. Either they feel they are enjoying everything that married folks enjoy, so there is no reason to marry; they are afraid that by marrying they will ruin a good thing; or they are beginning to have conflicting feelings about the relationship, though not enough to break up. In the case of the last reason, the relationship may be losing some of its luster or is obviously not healthy. But when the couple ventures to discuss the possibility of dissolving the union, it hurts terribly, leaving them paralyzed, and they continue to stay together with no concrete plans for the future.

In a prolonged relationship, couples do tend to believe that they are already enjoying most of the benefits of marriage. They have a regular sexual partner and the comforts of monogamy. They can depend upon having a familiar companion for events, parties, and recreational activities. They don't have to worry about impressing a new date or going through the often self-conscious period of getting to know a new person. If they are cohabiting, they have someone with whom to share expenses and household duties and someone to come home to at night. Except for having children, which even today most people still believe should be within the institution of marriage, couples who over time are reluctant to marry just can't see any advantage to making their relationship legal. In fact, they sometimes still hold onto the fact that they have it all, and should their relationship turn sour, they could get out of it without having to go through the pain of divorce. They haven't bargained for the fact that in all likelihood their hearts have already married, making marriage almost seem unnecessary. The problem is that almost always, at least one member of the couple will eventually want to marry and because their hearts have already unconsciously taken that step, any attempt to sever the relationship will result in the same pain, loneliness, and doubt as a divorce. In the end, it is never easy to end a *heart marriage*, which often causes couples to give in and marry to avoid the heartache. Many times this plunge into marriage is made without the articulated commitment to spend a lifetime together or a discussion of the important issues that face married couples. Since their hearts are married and they have been together for so long, those discussions may appear unnecessary. However, such open and pointed discussions are an important step in establishing a healthy marriage.

Another reason that couples are reluctant to marry over time is that they are truly afraid that marriage could ruin a good thing. In today's culture, it is likely that one or both of the individuals come from divorced families and have watched many of their friends marry and divorce. Though it may still be a hoped-for ideal, they have little confidence in the institution of marriage. And because their hearts are married, they don't feel compelled to legally marry. They already have the intimacy they desire and are comfortable leaving it just as it is. Again, almost inevitably at least one person in the relationship will begin to think about starting a family or perhaps begin to feel the need for more financial or emotional security and will want to marry. Many times that person will put pressure on the other to marry and in order not to feel the loneliness of separation, the couple will indeed proceed to the altar without confronting the underlying feeling of fear that is creating the reluctance. When fear keeps the heart married couple from lawfully marrying, it is best to seek the help of a therapist and begin to talk through the important issues surrounding the fear and reluctance. The fear doesn't magically disappear and these issues cannot be resolved without honest discussion. Failure to confront these issues before marriage can result in resentment later and lay the groundwork for a self-fulfilling prophesy that ultimately leads to the very divorce that the couple feared.

The third reason that there may be reluctance to marry over time is that the relationship is troubled. There may be disagreement and arguments, the positive feelings may begin to fade over time, or the couple may begin to see things in each other that create an underlying sense of dissatisfaction. Without giving voice to it, one or both persons in the relationship may realize that there are basic differences that would cause great difficulty in a marriage. These could be differences in religion, money management, the desire to have children, or simply ambition and the kind of life each wants to enjoy. Whatever the dissatisfaction, it creates a reluctance to marry that is well founded, but sometimes not openly stated or even recognized. Along with the reluctance, however, is also the inability to sever the relationship and the feeling of being stuck. This reluctance to marry, but inability to break up is most likely because the couple is heart married and without knowing it, is so bound to each other that breaking up feels like getting a divorce. The couple may entertain the idea of separating and do so for a time, but they often misinterpret the pain they experience when they break up as proof that they love each other and should be together. The couple is experiencing the normal feelings of loss, sadness, and devastation that occur when two intimately bound people sever a relationship. Unfortunately, rather than realizing that the dissolution is warranted and the pain inevitable under the circumstances, the couple moves in the opposite direction and decides that perhaps they should marry after all.

REMEMBER ALICE AND JAMES

Alice and James were introduced in chapter 1. They are a particularly good example of the reluctance to marry over time as a sign of *heart marriage*. The couple met during their first semester in college and dated for seven years before marrying. At first it was perfectly understandable that they would delay marriage until they finished college. Both were ambitious, and family expectations included college graduation. Then, however, there just never seemed to be the perfect time. Even after they graduated and began to attend the weddings of friends, there was always a reason to wait. First, it was applying for graduate school, then finishing graduate school, and finally getting settled in their careers. Taken at face value, all of these seem to be good reasons, but for Alice and James there was a reluctance that they never really put their fingers on and could not quite articulate. Often when couples have been together over time, their hearts have married, so unconsciously, legal marriage seems redundant, creating a hesitancy to marry that even they don't fully understand.

Upon closer examination, at least two of the reasons described in this chapter are operating in the case of Alice and James. First of all, this couple did seem to be already enjoying all of the benefits of marriage. They were sexual partners, monogamous, and were considered by all of their friends and even their families to be a solid couple. They moved to the same city after college graduation so that they could be together and even though they maintained separate residences, they spent most of their nights together, vacationed with family, and traveled together. It is easy to see that there was not much left for them to do that would require them to marry, except start a family. Although they talked about it as they watched their friends marry, in the end it was only at the urging and advice of his parents that James finally proposed to Alice and presented her with an engagement ring. Perhaps the fact that they were, "acting like a married couple" in almost every way paradoxically put getting married on the back burner.

The other reason for their reluctance to marry is evident when one looks closely at the relationship. Particularly once Alice and James finished college, there were telltale signs of some major differences between them in terms of how they saw their future and what they wanted out of life. Over time, their sexual relationship wasn't as exciting, making the areas in which they were not compatible more obvious. Alice was more career-oriented and wanted James to be more ambitious. James felt that Alice was compulsive and wanted her to loosen up. Alice was idealistic and had a desire to make a difference. James didn't really appreciate her fervor and even preferred that she spend less time in volunteer activities. After the marriage, they couldn't agree on such important issues as when to have children, how to manage their money, and the division of labor.

In the case of Alice and James who had a seven-year relationship before marriage, it would be reasonable to think that these issues would have been discussed and these areas of disagreement confronted. However, remember that *heart marriage* is the unintentional binding together of two people who care for each other. It often occurs before the couple gets around to such discussions about the future and the realistic issues that face couples who choose to spend and share their lives in marriage. *Heart marriage* is emotionally intense and the couples are intimately tied together, but since there is no concrete and stated commitment, they may feel vulnerable and therefore overlook differences that could threaten the relationship. Sometimes they may recognize that differences exist but fail to confront them. Often, by the time a couple begins to think about the issues that are important in marriage, such as having and raising a family, handling money, planning for the future, and religious preferences, *heart marriage* has already taken place and the couple puts energy into holding the relationship together rather than determining whether it has lasting qualities for the long haul.

In conclusion, in a prolonged relationship, the reluctance to marry over time, in conjunction with sexual intimacy, monogamy, and cohabitation, is a sign that *heart marriage* has most likely taken place. Likewise, when one member of a couple ultimately desires to formalize the relationship by marrying, this feeling of "being stuck" is a sign that something must surely change if the relationship is to continue and thrive. For this reason, reluctance to marry over time is referred to as the pivotal sign. At this point, a couple needs to assess their relationship and openly state their intentions for a future together. If they both desire to make a permanent commitment to each other, but have fears and issues they are willing to face together, the couple would likely benefit from counseling. If they cannot do this, or if both individuals are not on the same page, then dissolution of the relationship, a *heart divorce*, is the healthiest choice. Too often the couple takes neither of these paths. They ignore the signs, and because it seems like the easiest or most reasonable solution after investing so much time together, they decide they might as well get married.

Because the dissolution of *heart marriage* is often as painful as legal divorce, it is a hard choice for couples to make. However, finding ways to discuss and be prepared for this difficult process will produce more constructive decisions. We have referred to the ending of a *heart marriage* throughout these chapters as a *heart divorce*. Many heart married couples who reached that pivotal point in their relationship and chose the wedding path find themselves in counseling on the brink of divorce, knowing that they should never have married and wishing they had effectively heart divorced instead of walked down the aisle. Equally as confusing, are the heart married couples who finally sever their relationship and experience a *heart divorce* without realizing and understanding the intensity of such dissolution. It leaves them wondering why they are experiencing such sadness, pain, and heartache long after the breakup. The dissolution is especially devastating when an individual continues to carry all the emotional baggage that accompanies these situations and it then negatively impacts future relationships.

Because a *heart divorce* is often the best alternative for couples and could save them the devastation of a failed marriage, the next chapter will address this concept. It will outline four signs that indicate that a *heart marriage* is troubled and very likely doomed to failure. By recognizing these signs, couples will also be able to recognize in their own *heart marriage* when a *heart divorce* is the healthiest choice.

Taking It to Heart: A Call to Action

❤   If you have been in your relationship for a long time and you or your partner appear to be more and more reluctant to marry over time, find a place to be alone and write down the reasons you give yourself for not wanting to marry or the reasons your partner gives you for his/her reluctance.

❤   Ask yourself honestly if you want a future with your girl/boyfriend and whether you know for sure if your partner wants a future with you.

❤   After you have done this, whether your answer is yes or no, set a time to discuss this openly and honestly with your partner and ask him/her to be open and honest with you.

❤   If you determine that you both really do want a future together, begin to tackle the obstacles keeping you "stuck." If either of you answers no, then pay careful attention to the next chapters on *heart divorce*.

7

How to Recognize the Signs

Do You Need a Heart Divorce?

IN CHAPTER 2 YOU were introduced to Debbie and Mike, a couple who moved from a *heart marriage* into a legal marriage that ended in a painful divorce. If we examine this relationship, there were many indications prior to their marriage that instead of a legal marriage, this relationship needed a dissolution or *heart divorce*. Like many couples in similar situations, they had attempted to break up several times only to be drawn back together. Each mistook the comfort of sex and the pain of separation for love, and assumed they loved each other enough to marry. It is not unusual for couples to attempt to fix their *heart marriage* by making it legal. They know that there are troubled spots in their relationship, but do not recognize them for what they are—signals that they need a *heart divorce*.

DO YOU NEED A HEART DIVORCE?

Just as there are indicators to help identify the development of a *heart marriage*, there are behaviors to indicate the need for a *heart divorce*. These behaviors or thoughts may be red flags that show the relationship is not healthy. By definition, *heart divorce* is simply *the formal and clearly articulated and agreed upon dissolution of heart marriage*. The signs and symptoms of a troubled *heart marriage* are often very similar to those seen in a legal marriage.

Sign 1: Unresolved Arguments and Disagreements

While occasional conflict is to be expected in every relationship, there are both healthy and destructive ways to solve these problems. In *heart marriage*, because the intentional commitment has not been made, differences can be hard to settle. There are several unproductive ways disagreements may be dealt with in a *heart marriage*. The first is through heated verbal exchanges that bring up old issues in addition to the new issues. The verbal exchanges may be laced with anger and get personal such as "fighting dirty." Often, these couples tell themselves that because they are not married, they are free to say anything under the guise of being honest. Fighting that gets personal is very hurtful and real issues are often lost in the heat of the moment. "Fighting dirty," or fighting that gets personal, means the person's value and worth are impugned. It may include name-calling and character attacks. Further, such verbal attacks are a clear indication that there is worse to come. It must be stated that physical violence should never be tolerated and is rarely an isolated incident, but "fighting dirty" can also have long term effects. Such verbal assaults can become a pattern of verbal abuse, which destroys relationships and is harmful to an individual's sense of well being and confidence.

On the other hand, one or both of the partners in the *heart marriage* may try to avoid confrontation altogether and, in so doing, completely avoid the discussion of differences and disagreements. There is fear that the relationship is not stable and that the other person is free to walk away since they are not married. The couple may feel it is too risky to confront the difficulties, so they just hope time will resolve the problems. Thus, issues that need to be discussed and resolved never get aired. This is very unhealthy both to the relationship and to the individuals because it impedes honesty and openness, which are essential for a fulfilling marriage. Further, important issues are almost certain to resurface eventually, often made worse by years of unspoken hurt that turns into resentment that is difficult to reverse.

Finally, there is a third type of arguing that is often ignored by the couple, but is actually a signal that the relationship is ailing. This is continuous or constant bickering over everyday things that may be rather insignificant or that actually could be resolved with fairly simple compromises. Bickering becomes a regular method of communication that may unconsciously signal trouble that the couple is unwilling to confront. It can become a way to avoid dealing with the underlying, yet more important, realization that there are substantial differences between the couple that threaten the relationship. Constant bickering can conceal the real truth that the feelings they once shared, which resulted in their *heart marriage*, do not represent the kind of love that can sustain the relationship over time. Constant bickering creates an unhealthy tension and begins to pull the couple apart. Unfortunately since it typically doesn't deal with the real issues, the couple often blows it off as the result of normal everyday stresses. In fact, sometimes, the bickering becomes a way to connect, although an unhealthy one, and is followed by making up with affection and sex. Again, the problem is that the underlying issues don't simply go away; they will eventually come to the surface mightily, demanding to be resolved. In most cases where constant bickering becomes almost an accepted part of the relationship, the healthiest resolution on the front end is a *heart divorce*.

All three behaviors—fighting dirty, avoidance of confrontation, and constant bickering over relatively unimportant issues—are habits that are difficult to break without professional intervention. They are serious barriers to lasting intimacy and signals of an unhealthy relationship. If any of these three styles of conflict resolution is practiced repeatedly, the couple may need a *heart divorce*.

Sign 2: Frequent Thoughts of Leaving

In a legal marriage, the vows and promises are made either before a judge and witnesses or a minister/priest and a church full of people. These vows usually include a declaration that the participants intend to stay married "in sickness and in health, for richer or poorer, for better or worse." They frequently include the promise to stay married "till death do us part." While the making of these promises publicly does not insure they will not be broken, it does signify a willingness to be in partnership through life, including during the difficult times.

In *heart marriage*, though the couple is definitely bound together, these declarations have not been made, thus there may be a feeling of uncertainty and vulnerability concerning the dedication of participants. In fact, sometimes before the relationship evolves into *heart marriage*, it starts with the thought that if it doesn't work, one can simply leave without the pain and messiness of divorce. What the couple doesn't realize or consider at that time, is the fact that once they become heart married, dissolving the relationship isn't that easy and carries with it all the pain of divorce. Therefore, it is important to recognize and be aware that if either individual entertains frequent thoughts of leaving the relationship, this is a sign of trouble and a red flag that should not be ignored. It signals a lack of the clearly stated commitment that is important to weather the normal ups and downs of a relationship.

Still another facet that is equally telling and disturbing is the worry on the part of one member of the couple that the other person is planning or wanting to leave. This thought can become a general undercurrent that is unsettling as it results in feelings of insecurity. The couple may even speak of breaking up and try to discern what this would mean and how their lives would look. Each time an argument occurs, one or both individuals may threaten to leave or ask the other to leave, further creating instability and eroding the relationship.

If this separation talk happens frequently or if the thought of leaving, even though unspoken, begins to occur regularly, the couple may need a *heart divorce*. When one or both people consider leaving the relationship often, there is a sense of insecurity that the relationship is not steady. In fact, the relationship is inherently unsettled because no formal commitment has been made. Living with a sense of uncertainty about the status of the relationship is not healthy emotionally. Couples who frequently consider leaving the relationship or who worry that their partner wants to leave may need a *heart divorce*.

Sign 3: Inability to Plan for the Future

In a *heart marriage*, the couple is intimately bound together and exhibits the behaviors of marriage but has made no intentional decision nor come to a stated agreement to marry. Healthy relationships require open and candid discussion about the future. If either person resists planning for the future or cannot commit to the future, the *heart marriage* may need to be terminated. Often, the couple can avoid talking about the future for a bit and will attempt to be content with a relationship that is just lived "one day at a time." However, most heart married couples will eventually want to discuss the subject of children, legal marriage, and the acquisition of property, among other things. Other practical issues include designating power of attorney in case of serious illness and health care coverage and benefits.

Even for those people who don't appear to be worried or concerned about tomorrow, it is natural to eventually have some concern for what the future holds at least in general terms. It is likewise part of the natural progression of a maturing and healthy relationship to make plans together and to want the emotional security of being able to depend upon your partner being a part of your life over time. A large portion of that sense of security comes from being able to talk about and articulate what the future will look like. Certainly, the passing time makes these discussions, particularly about children and property, a practical matter as well as an emotional one. If one or both of the participants is unable or unwilling to discuss the future of the relationship or their commitment to the relationship in concrete terms this raises a red flag that should not be ignored. The inability to make future plans may signal a lack of commitment or simply waning love within the relationship. It can also be an indication of more serious emotional issues and fears that hamper the ability of one of the individuals to make an authentic emotional connection. When that is the case, the situation may require the professional guidance of a therapist in order for change to take place. In any event, the inability to plan for the future is a roadblock to a healthy relationship and indicates that it may be appropriate for the relationship to be dissolved rather than continuing to wait for an unlikely outcome.

Sign 4: General Sense of Unease

Sometimes, the couple in a *heart marriage* will experience a general sense of discomfort with the living arrangements and the direction of the relationship. Because *heart marriage* occurs without intentionality, the relationship may just flounder along. It is neither good nor bad exactly, but there is a feeling that something is not right. Quite often, sexual intimacy is the one piece of the relationship that still feels good. The couple can try to ignore other warning signs because sex provides the feeling of connection even if just briefly. Over time, it is difficult to maintain a relationship based only on the intimacy provided by sex.

The persistent general sense of unease is difficult to describe, but will begin to affect the relationship as well as the individual experiencing it. It may manifest itself in feeling anxious or sad or simply not enjoying being with the partner. The person may feel as if there is nothing much to look forward to or talk about. It is often a nagging feeling that grows and becomes more apparent over time. If the general sense of dissatisfaction persists, like the other signals, it should not be ignored, and quite likely, a *heart divorce* is in order.

These four signs—unresolved arguments and disagreements, frequent thoughts of leaving the relationship, an inability to plan for the future, and a general sense of unease—should alert either person in the *heart marriage* that the relationship is in danger. If a couple has one or more of these indicators, the couple needs to assess the state of the relationship. It might be helpful to confide in a friend or other support person that *heart marriage* has taken place and that it is not working. Once the concept of *heart marriage* is understood, it is easier for support systems to provide the needed emotional strength to weather the *heart divorce*. *Heart marriage* does not have to end in *heart divorce*, but *heart marriage* does have to be transformed in order for the relationship to survive and thrive. *Heart divorce* can be as painful as a legal divorce but if the relationship is not right and cannot be repaired, it is better to get a *heart divorce* than to pursue a legal marriage. In the event of a *heart divorce*, the couple must do the hard work of separation and dissolution in order for the process of healing to take place.

DEBBIE AND MIKE REVISITED

Looking again at Debbie and Mike, all four of the signs were there for a *heart divorce*. Their relationship was described as volatile. They fought often and Mike blamed it on his artistic temperament. Frequent fighting in a relationship is a clear sign that something is wrong. Rarely does fighting improve after a couple marries.

During the relationship, Debbie often thought of leaving and did, in fact, break up with Mike several times, only to be lured back by the comfort of sex. Those thoughts and attempts to end the relationship were signals that Debbie was unsure and that the relationship was not healthy. They were clear indications of a general sense of unease and though she consulted a therapist, she ultimately pushed them out of her mind, likely because it was so painful to leave.

Finally, they were not able to make plans to marry seemingly because Mike did not have stable employment and therefore was not willing to marry Debbie, although he did feel love for her. In fact, it appears that the marriage ultimately came about with very little planning, and was, for the most part, a response to the prolonged time that they had been together and their inability to break up without being drawn back to each other. Debbie and Mike needed a *heart divorce*, but were unable to see it at the time. Had they been able to recognize it and work through the pain of such a dissolution they could have saved themselves additional heartache. Sadly, as is most often the case, the signs persisted after the couple married and then with the availability of a legal and articulated avenue to end the marriage, they did so with a divorce.

If a couple realizes their *heart marriage* cannot transition into a healthy marriage, they must do the difficult work of *heart divorce*. There are steps that can be taken to heal the broken hearts and prevent the tendency to repeat the same mistakes over and over again. The next chapter will explore how to navigate *heart divorce*. First, this Heart Divorce Quiz can assist a couple in determining whether *a heart divorce* is warranted in their relationship. Take it now and see for yourself.

HEART DIVORCE QUIZ:
DO YOU NEED A HEART DIVORCE?

Directions: Answer yes or no to the following questions about your relationship.

1. Do you and your partner have at least one heated verbal exchange everyday?

2. Do you avoid confronting your partner about issues you disagree on?

3. Do you constantly bicker over the small things of daily life?

4. Do you often think about breaking up or leaving your partner?

5. Do you worry that your partner wants to leave the relationship?

6. Do either of you verbally threaten to leave the relationship more than once a month?

7. Do you have an uneasy feeling that the relationship is just not healthy?

8. Do you rarely, or never, talk honestly and calmly about issues such as marriage, children, or buying house, including specific timeframes?

9. Do either you or your partner want to get legally married but the other one is reluctant?

10. Are you afraid to tell your partner what you want in a relationship?

Scoring Key

❤ If you answered yes to five questions, it is possible that you need a *heart divorce*.

❤ If you answered yes to eight or more questions, you definitely need a *heart divorce*, or at the very least, you need to seriously evaluate your relationship and improve the quality and dynamics of interaction with your partner.

Taking It to Heart: A Call to Action

❤ Make a personal decision to stop arguing. If your partner begins to bicker, simply state that you have chosen not to argue with him/her. An argument cannot take place when only one person participates.

❤ When you have thoughts of leaving, stop and make a list of what is troubling you about the relationship. Be as specific as possible and set a time to discuss it with your boy/girlfriend.

❤ Keep a log/journal of each time: a) you think about breaking up; b) you or your partner threatens to leave; c) you feel hesitant or fearful or uneasy about your relationship.

❤ After taking these three steps for a month, if arguments persist; if your partner is unwilling to discuss your concerns or you are unsuccessful in addressing them productively; and if you find that you are making entries in your journal at least every day or two, it is time to take the steps outlined in chapter 8 of *My Heart Got Married And I Didn't Know It.*

8

How to Navigate Heart Divorce

*Make the Decision, Take Action, Heal
and Move Forward*

THOUGH MANY MARRIAGES ARE over before the judge makes the final declaration, it is the legal divorce decree that marks the formal end to a marriage and clears the way for the couple to move forward. The symbolic removal of the wedding ring, the separation of residence, and the conspicuous appearance in public without one's mate are all steps in a dying relationship, but it is the uttered words, "our divorce is final," that, at last, put the marriage to rest.

Divorce is the legal dissolution of a marriage. It comes about via an intentional decision, perhaps initiated by one partner, but ultimately, even if only from a legal standpoint, agreed upon by both. It carries with it the division of property, the provision for financial compensation, and the assignment of custody and visitation rights when children are involved. It can mean the return of the female's maiden name, or with increasing frequency, the removal of the hyphenated last name for both partners. Divorce rarely comes about without a great deal of soul searching, discussion, tears, and planning of next steps. There can be a considerable length of time between the decision and legal declaration. The gravity of divorce is uniformly recognized and is often compared to a death, as it marks the end of an intimately bound union, a legal partnership, and a life's dream.

Divorce rates in the United States are typically cited at around 40 percent, indicating that we can expect almost one out of two marriages will end in divorce. The actual divorce rate in America, however, is difficult to compute because not all states collect the data and there are a number of variables such as race, ethnic group, and socioeconomic status. Nevertheless, a "National Survey of Family Growth" most recently reports that 33 percent of first marriages end in separation or divorce within ten years and 43 percent within fifteen years based on a study of women ages fifteen to forty-four. (Centers for Disease Control, "National Survey," sec. 2, lines 9–14) Most literature that considers the subject of divorce cites the 40 to 50 percent statistic. Regardless of the absolute accuracy of the number, it is clear that the divorce rate is high, and though apparently remaining fairly level the last few years, has risen steadily since the 1950s (Centers for Disease Control, "National Survey," sec. 2.)

In fact, many young adults use the divorce rate as the rationale for their decision to cohabit before marriage or instead of marrying at all. As noted previously, studies indicate that cohabitation rarely protects couples from the pain of divorce. Since cohabitation together with sexual intimacy and monogamy can cause the heart to marry, severing that relationship will be accompanied by most, if not all, of the heart wrenching emotions of divorce. With divorce, a couple has made the intentional decision to end the marriage and anticipates the anguish, hurt, and loneliness that most certainly will occur. Participants recognize the emotions for what they are and know that it will take time to heal. There are books to read, support groups to attend, divorce counselors to engage, and a great deal of empathy and support from friends and family.

In contrast, when a heart married couple decides to separate, the same emotions occur as in divorce, yet there is no formalized process. There are no books or articles to draw upon and often friends and family, who have had either spoken or unspoken reservations about the relationship, are silently cheering and offering platitudes such as "This is for the best," or "You'll meet someone else soon and be fine," or "Aren't you glad this happened before you got married?" The emotions that predictably come with separation, combined with the lack of a formalized process and less than helpful support, often backfires and causes the couple to mistake what they are going through as proof that they must love each other. They resume their relationship and many times decide that since they can't live without each other, they will go ahead and get married.

What these couples actually need is a formalized process that will help them to anticipate the emotions that accompany ending their relationship, recognize them for what they are, and take the necessary steps to heal and move forward with their lives. We introduced this concept in chapter 1 and called it *heart divorce*. *Heart divorce* is defined as the formal and clearly articulated and agreed upon dissolution of *heart marriage*. In chapter 7, we discussed the four signs that indicate that a *heart divorce* may be warranted. They are unresolved arguments and disagreements, frequent thoughts of leaving, inability to plan for the future, and a general sense of unease. Almost always when a heart married couple contemplates separation and ultimately does dissolve their relationship, one or more of these signs have been present in the relationship for quite some time. Assuming that at least one of the partners in the *heart marriage* is experiencing these troubling signs, the remainder of this chapter will outline a process to give couples the tools and confidence needed to navigate a *heart divorce*.

STEP ONE:
FIRST THINGS FIRST—ACKNOWLEDGE
YOU ARE HEART MARRIED

In order to make good decisions in the midst of *heart marriage*, the first step is to acknowledge your situation. Consider your relationship in light of the signs we have discussed: sexual intimacy, monogamy, cohabitation, and the reluctance to marry. Admit that your heart has married without your knowing it. By acknowledging this, you can understand why you feel stuck and emotionally committed to the relationship in the face of so many signs of trouble. It is also important to realize that your feeling and declaration, whether silent or verbalized, that the relationship isn't going anywhere is an admission that you have become dissatisfied with being in a static place with no stated future. It is critical for you to understand that your choices at this point are to stay the same, which is clearly not healthy, or to move forward either by intentionally improving the relationship and transitioning into a marriage, or by dissolving it with similar purpose and care. Just as in a marriage, improving your relationship will take real effort and leaving it will be difficult and painful. This admission will help prepare you for the road ahead. In a later chapter we will discuss improving the relationship and transitioning into marriage, but at this point we will continue to concentrate on executing a *heart divorce*.

STEP TWO:
IDENTIFY WHAT YOU NEED IN A LASTING RELATIONSHIP AND MAKE AN HONEST ASSESSMENT OF YOUR PRESENT SITUATION

Now that you have acknowledged that you are heart married and that your relationship is showing signs that dissolution may be warranted, it is critical that you thoughtfully identify what you are looking for and need in a lasting relationship. You may have done this informally at some time or you may believe you know what you want; however, it is extremely helpful to take the time not only to think seriously about this, but also to put it on paper so that you can continue to refer to it as you progress. This assessment must be done alone and should take place before you discuss it with your partner. Although it is difficult to use reason with decisions of the heart, by doing so you are poised to take responsibility for your decisions rather than be a passive victim of emotions. When you talk with your partner, you need to be prepared so that you can communicate with confidence and clarity. To that end, list those things that are most important to you in regard to the future, identify the type person with whom you wish to spend your life, and delineate the specific ways in which you wish to be treated. When you finish the list, go back and ask yourself which of the items are nonnegotiable and which could be compromised. Focus at this time on the nonnegotiables.

Now compare the items on the list to your present relationship and determine where you are. If you have been completely honest with yourself, it should be clear to you whether your present relationship holds promise for providing the future you desire. It will become obvious to you if the relationship isn't right and should be ended. It is possible that you will discover that the relationship isn't dead, but that in order to feel comfortable you need to address your issues, formalize your commitment to each other through marriage, and begin to make plans for your life together. Your list will help you identify those unresolved issues. In contrast to the unplanned and unintentional way your *heart marriage* evolved, this step begins an intentional process of deciding about your future.

STEP THREE:
COMMUNICATE OPENLY WITH YOUR PARTNER

Armed with the clarity of your assessment, it is time to communicate your thoughts and feelings openly with your partner. Admit that although there has been no proposal, no ring, and no wedding, you realize your heart has married, binding you together emotionally in the same way that lawfully married couples are bound. Express honestly that you feel uncomfortable about how the relationship is going and at the same time recognize that you are "stuck," unable to move forward, yet unable to separate. Share your assessment of what you want in a lasting relationship and how your relationship compares to that. Ask your partner for an honest and open response in return.

This communication will open the door to dealing with your relationship with intentionality and help you to take charge of your future. It could be that you both are having the same feelings of unrest and you will agree immediately that the relationship needs to be severed. It could also be that you are on different pages altogether, one wanting to be married and the other still not sure, or even worse, viewing it as a passing love affair or convenient partnership. It could also turn out that you both recognize that although you care for each other deeply, you have issues and fears keeping you paralyzed, and by acknowledging this you can begin to confront these issues. It is not necessary that the two of you be in exactly the same place, but it is necessary that you know and respect where each is in regard to the relationship, present and future, so that you can make decisions intentionally about the next steps.

STEP FOUR:
DECIDE UPON AN INTENTIONAL PLAN
TO MOVE FORWARD

You've openly communicated where you are in your relationship and where you think you want to go and now you must take action. Different scenarios require different courses, but in all cases, it is important that you begin to act purposefully to move the relationship from its static position. Depending upon your partner's willingness and desire for the future, you may have to act alone. It is important that you take responsibility for your feelings, your decisions, and your actions, and ask for honesty on the part of your partner in taking responsibility for the same.

Scenario 1: You know the heart marriage must end.

When you are sure that the *heart marriage* does not offer the lifelong relationship that you desire, you must take responsibility to end it. The best course of action is to be forthright and honest with your partner. Share your understanding of how you have become bound together and how this makes it extremely difficult to separate, and at the same time, discuss the reasons that you cannot see a lasting future together. It will take time to heal after making the break. The following suggestions can help you get through the process.

UNDERSTAND, ANTICIPATE, AND OWN THE PREDICTABLE FEELINGS.

Understand that ending your *heart marriage* will bring intense feelings, just as surely as if you were married. You have been monogamous and sexually intimate and that creates a strong bond. More than likely you have cohabited or spent most of your nights and free time together, and though reluctant to marry, have been unable to pull yourself apart. You may have initial feelings of relief, but beware that there are many other predictable emotions. Feeling guilt for hurting your partner is understandable, as are feelings of loneliness. Often you feel lost and afraid about your future and whether or not you are doing the right thing. It will feel strange to be single and you may be uncomfortable around the opposite sex. Second thoughts about your ability to choose the right partner and create a healthy relationship and marriage are common. Moreover, you likely will truly miss each other. These are normal feelings and are not an indication that you should be together. Rather, they are the result of being intimately bound in *heart marriage* with a person whom you have cared for deeply.

FIND A WAY TO FORMALIZE THIS PROCESS.

Just as removing the wedding ring is a ritual that signals the end of a marriage, it is also helpful to identify a ritual ending to your relationship, such as setting a time when you will put away pictures or special mementos. You might consider listing in writing possessions that were purchased together or gifts that have special meaning and formally decide upon how to distribute them. If you are cohabiting, avoid running out in a huff or dragging out the moving process. Set a specific date that all belongings of the one who will leave the residence are packed and removed. As a formalizing ritual, you may even write your own dissolution statement and file it just as you would a divorce petition. This statement can be respectful of your partner, but it must clearly state the reason for the ultimate separation.

Verbalize and give voice to what you are experiencing.

You may want to share with others that although you know you have made the necessary decision, it feels very much like a divorce. If friends or family offer platitudes that reveal that they are unaware of what you are going through, let them know that you understand that they mean well, but be honest about how difficult it has been to end the relationship and why. Let them know that you anticipate a grieving period and ask for their understanding. If you have second thoughts, bring out the list regarding your needs and how this relationship compared with those needs, then assert aloud that you are the only one who can claim a healthy future for yourself. Put a note where you see it daily that reminds you that it will take time to heal.

Develop a new routine with new activities to occupy your time.

This is a common and healthy coping mechanism for divorcing couples and is equally helpful in the case of *heart divorce*. Decide consciously to avoid the old places where you are likely to run into your partner. Give yourself space. This would be a good time to take a class, develop a new interest, and meet new people. There may be something that you have wanted to do for a long time, such as becoming involved in a hobby or taking a trip. Although you may not be able to do all of these things, it can be helpful to find one or two that best fits you.

Join a divorce recovery group and/or seek professional help.

If you find that you are still grieving just as intensely after several months, or that you are lapsing into depression, you may need help outside your family and friends. Understanding that you are going through a *heart divorce*, you may want to join a divorce recovery group. Sharing with others in similar situations can provide the kind of support needed to produce healing. It is often necessary to have the objective perspective of a professional therapist through individual counseling. Moreover, there may be other underlying fears and feelings that surface, such as insecurity, damaged self-esteem, or resentment that must be resolved before you can be healthy and move forward.

Scenario 2: You want to marry, but your partner isn't interested.

Once you can admit to yourself that you want to marry and have a future together but your partner is on a different page, you may have to make the difficult decision alone to leave the relationship. Avoid the temptation to present your decision as an ultimatum such as "either we need to get married or break up." That ultimatum often leads to marriage out of frustration or fear of losing each other, when the truth is that this decision is not an either/or proposition. Only one can be correct. In this case you have determined that you wish to marry. That is your decision, but you are not sure what your partner wants. So rather than an ultimatum, simply communicate honestly to your partner that you desire to marry and ask for an honest response. If your partner responds that he/she is not ready or willing to marry, then you must make the decision that is in your best interest. For your own emotional health, you must decide to sever the relationship and give yourself the opportunity to heal and over time find someone who will share your goals and desires.

The same steps for moving through the process in the first scenario, also apply to this scenario. It is desirable to *anticipate, understand, and own your feelings; formalize the dissolution; verbalize and give voice to what you are experiencing; develop a new routine with new activities; and perhaps, seek professional help.* Dissolution in this situation will be even harder, because you have owned your desire to marry and have a future with your partner. Now that you have opened communication and asked for honesty from your partner, you have learned what you were likely afraid to know, but already suspected. You now must admit that your partner does not share your desire.

In anticipating and owning your feelings, realize that you are not only hurt, but you may also feel stupid or foolish for not recognizing the situation or for waiting so long to act. It is best to acknowledge this and understand that your situation and resultant feelings are more common than you think. You have not been stupid, rather you have been heart married, intimately bound to a person you have cared for deeply. It is hard to end such a relationship.

You will also benefit by determining a way to formalize the dissolution. Once you know that your partner does not have the same desire for the relationship, it may take you some time to put finality to it, but you will want to set for yourself a timeline as a boundary. It doesn't have to be a hard and fast due date, but it does need to be a reasonably close timeframe. You may need to confide in a trusted friend not only for support but also to hold you accountable for following through on your decision. In the meantime, do not try to convince, cajole, or manipulate your partner. It may work in the short run and result in a wedding, but it will be doomed in the long run. You have expressed yourself. Your partner knows your position and should act out of his/her own conviction, just as you are doing.

It is helpful to give voice and verbalize your situation for what it is, a painful *heart divorce*. Name and own this with your friends and family. Let them know what is happening and ask them for the kind of support you need. In this case, it may be helpful to see a therapist early in the process. Because you have made a decision that reflects your best interest but is in conflict with what your heart wants, professional help may be even more important. It can help you keep your resolve and gain the confidence you need to go through with the *heart divorce* so that you can begin a new and more productive future.

Scenario 3: You both want a future together,
but have paralyzing issues and fears.

Remember, the assumption in this chapter is that the signs indicating the need for a *heart divorce* are present in your relationship. In this scenario, however, after assessing what you want as compared to your present relationship, you both believe that you do love and desire a future with each other, but have paralyzing issues and fears. Given this, the first and most productive step is to seek professional help. Within the context of professional counseling, you will be able to determine what those issues and fears are and work to resolve them.

It should be noted that counseling in this situation is different from the usual premarriage counseling for a couple who has decided to marry. Typical premarriage counseling is designed to fortify the couple's relationship and bring out common issues that all married couples must confront, as well as give the couple an opportunity to express any normal fears and doubts they may have. Premarriage counseling is encouraged for all couples who are contemplating marriage or for engaged couples who are in the midst of planning their wedding. In fact, many churches and individual ministers require premarriage counseling. Similarly, it is becoming more common for the government to encourage premarriage counseling, with many states offering reductions in marriage license fees or other such incentives.

The counseling suggested for the heart married couple who recognizes there are issues but still believes they want to marry is somewhat different. It may cover some of the same ground, but it is clear that counseling will address a troubled relationship. That is not to say that the issues cannot be resolved satisfactorily, but beware that when a couple is already experiencing difficulties that warrant professional counseling before marriage, that is a danger signal in itself. Marriage does not improve a problematic relationship. The purpose of counseling in this case is to discuss both the obvious issues that have arisen over the years as well as the underlying reasons the couple has exhibited reluctance to marry and plan for the future.

The couple may find that these fears and issues can be resolved and a future together secured. It is equally possible that through counseling they will realize that although their hearts have married and are intricately bound together, the relationship is unhealthy. It may become clear that their relationship never transitioned to an intentional discussion of needs, desires, and concrete hopes for the future. In this case, the fears and reluctance are well founded and are an indication of the need for a *heart divorce*. Regardless of the outcome of counseling, if the couple is honest and conscientious in the process, they will leave the experience with a sense of direction and be prepared to make an intentional decision about the future of their relationship.

Scenario 4: Your partner leaves you unexpectedly or without warning.

There are times in *heart marriage,* just like in any other relationship, when one person decides to break up. This often is unexpected and sudden. Sometimes there is infidelity or one partner has turned the frequent thoughts of leaving into action without openly communicating this to the other. Still other times there have been many previous threats with no follow through. Regardless of the reason, the sudden termination of the relationship is painful. When this happens, it is time to do your own assessment even in the face of turmoil and strong emotions. The result of such an assessment will typically produce realization that danger signs have been present for a long time and the *heart marriage* has not been healthy, if for no other reason than because it occurred without the intentional decision of the partners. All of the steps and strategies outlined in this chapter apply to this situation as well and can help get you through the unexpected *heart divorce*.

MARTHA SUE AND RANDY

Martha Sue and Randy knew each other nearly all of their lives, but it was not until half way through college that they began to date. The relationship got serious fairly quickly and sexual intimacy soon followed. This was the first serious relationship for both of them. They continued to date throughout their pharmacy studies and Randy entered practice one year before Martha Sue. When Martha Sue started pharmacy school in the same city, it just seemed to make sense to share an apartment. They had similar schedules, went to the same school, and were basically spending most of their nights together anyway. Randy had a very close family and Martha Sue attended all the family functions, holidays, summer vacations, and weekend outings just as if she were Randy's wife. Soon after Randy started his practice and Martha Sue graduated, he bought a house and she moved in. Everyone thought this would be the time they would marry, but it didn't happen. Because he bought the house, to be fair, she bought the furniture. Though not married, they certainly acted like a married couple. After five years, the family quit asking about marriage. They continued to wonder why no plans were being made and began to feel uneasy about the relationship. They tried not to be judgmental, but it just didn't make sense to them.

Without announcing it or knowing it, however, Randy and Martha Sue became heart married. Over time, they started to take their relationship for granted and Martha Sue began to enjoy the attention she was getting from some of the pharmacy and medical students. She wondered if she had missed the fun of dating other people and noticed that between career and sports activities, Randy didn't have much time to dote on her. Randy, on the other hand, was comfortable with the relationship and believed that Martha Sue was satisfied. They had been together so long, Randy thought that she was okay with their routines.

Gradually, there were occasional arguments, but it came as a surprise to Randy when he found out Martha Sue was seeing someone else. He was devastated. They were sharing a home and expenses and even had joint property. Martha Sue had been a part of the family, and in the back of his mind, he always thought they would marry. They argued and cried and Randy felt anguish over the infidelity. Family and friends were consoled by the fact that this happened before marriage, but this provided little comfort for Randy. It was extremely hard to accept the infidelity and because of their living situation, separating was not that easy. Martha Sue began to be absent at family functions, but it took almost a year for Randy to tell his parents that they were going to split. Like many married couples they remained in the house together for a time, but were not in the same bedroom. Even though they were not married, it took almost two years for the dissolution to be complete.

Randy had a difficult time after the breakup and wasn't himself. He was noticeably quiet and out of sorts. The family was as supportive as they could be, but they really didn't know whether to be happy or sad. They did know that they wanted the best for their son and believed the breakup was for the best even though they hurt for him. They believed that time would heal and after awhile, Randy did begin to act normal again.

About that time Randy started going out with another pharmacist named Diane. They had known each other professionally and she had been a support for him through his breakup with Martha Sue. It seemed like an easy transition. In addition to being friends, the chemistry was electric and they became sexually active soon after officially starting to date. Although Randy had sold his house and rented an apartment, within a couple of months he was spending most of his nights at Diane's. This seemed to make sense because she lived quite a distance from him and it was just easier to stay than go home at the end of an evening. The relationship moved quickly, and again, Randy's heart married. He was crushed when after six months Diane came to him and said that she was not ready for a committed relationship. Once again, Randy moved everything that he had at Diane's back to his apartment. Terribly hurt, he began to doubt that he would find the person he was looking for and wondered if he was cut out for relationships. He poured himself into his work.

Even though they didn't identify it as such, Randy and Martha Sue were heart married and went through the painful process of *heart divorce*, which included dividing shared property. Martha Sue became involved with someone else and, though conflicted, wanted out of the relationship with Randy. The fact that it was not easy to separate is obvious in that it took them almost two years to actually move into separate residences. Randy's parents and family members were as supportive as they could be, but had mixed feelings themselves and certainly didn't know how to console him. Randy tried to handle the situation himself and did not bring others into it. Although it wasn't necessarily intentional, the time it took to divide their joint property, sell the house, and look for separate residences gave them some needed time to come to grips with the dissolution. Finally Randy seemed to get "over the hump" with the help of another relationship. Unfortunately, he followed a similar pattern with Diane, and seemed on his way to another *heart marriage*, when that relationship ended abruptly. It appears that though Randy certainly knew he loved Martha Sue and they had a long and committed relationship, he didn't recognize that he had been heart married, nor was he consciously aware of the behavior patterns that quite often marry the heart. In this post-sexual revolution era, early sexual involvement may be a cultural norm, but it can also be a first step in an unintended *heart marriage*. Had he seen this and acknowledged it, perhaps he would not have repeated that pattern with Diane. Going through the steps recommended in this chapter, particularly recognizing and acknowledging that his and Martha Sue's relationship was a *heart marriage* and all that goes with that realization would have assisted Randy in navigating his *heart divorce*. It would also have left him more aware and able to make sound behavioral choices in future relationships.

In summary, since *heart marriage* occurs without the intentional decision of the couple, the emotional binding happens before the couple knows it, which leaves them vulnerable to becoming "stuck" in a relationship that lacks the elements that lead to a lifetime commitment of loving behavior and growth. Often there are obvious signs that the relationship is unhealthy, but the couple feels unable to separate and mistakes their inability to break up for a signal that they should marry. Too many times, instead, the couple needs a *heart divorce*. When this occurs, if the couple together or individually will acknowledge their *heart marriage*; identify what they need in a lasting relationship and make an honest assessment of their present situation; communicate openly with their partner; and take intentional steps to move forward, they will be able to avoid a marriage that is likely to end in heartache. They will also be equipped to navigate a *heart divorce* for a healthier and more satisfying future. Some of these steps may seem unnecessary or too much trouble, but glossing over what is happening or thinking that healing will take care of itself can delay healthy adjustment and result in repeating old patterns in future relationships.

Although many of you have seen yourself in the descriptions given so far, there are hopefully some readers who are not presently in a *heart marriage* and want to keep it that way. In the next chapter, a straightforward approach for avoiding *heart marriage* altogether will be discussed. Before moving on, consider the following suggestions.

Taking It to Heart: A Call to Action

❤ If you believe that you need a *heart divorce*, now you have the tools to get through it. Set a deadline to formally begin this painful, but necessary, process. Give yourself some time to prepare, but don't set the deadline too far away. Waiting for Christmas, Valentine's Day, or a birthday to pass is just a "stalling" technique. Write your HD-Day on a piece of paper or calendar and put it where you can see it. You can do this!

❤ Go back and follow the four steps prescribed in this chapter. You have obviously already begun to go through Step One: "acknowledging that you are heart married" and Step Two: "assessing your present relationship," but it is equally important that you spend considerable time in the other half of Step Two: "identifying what you want in a lasting relationship." Now, make a list of what you have identified and put it where you can see it often. It's like any important goal, you have to be able to visualize it and see where you want to go in order to get there.

❤ Be sure that when you execute Step Three: "communicating openly with your partner," that you have already spent time with Step Four: "deciding upon a plan to move forward." There are times when Step Three holds some surprises, but you usually can predict fairly accurately what will happen, so be ready to execute your plan. It won't be easy, but remember—you can do this!

9

How to Avoid Heart Marriage

The Straight Answers You Need Now

B Y THIS POINT, YOU have a lot of thinking to do. As the reader, you find yourself in one of several possible positions. You may recognize that you are heart married and are bracing for the heartache that is likely to come in the near future. Or you realize you have experienced *heart marriage* in the past and for the first time really understand what happened. Maybe you have a friend or a family member who is in a *heart marriage* that is obviously unhealthy and you wish you could warn them about the pain that lies ahead. Or, you could be feeling relief that you are not presently in a *heart marriage* and are thinking that you never want to go though the pain and wasted time that are predictable results of such a relationship. Whichever your position, you are likely wondering if there is any way that *heart marriage* can be avoided and if so, how? Fortunately, even at this time of shifting moral standards, changing norms for couples, and more young adults delaying marriage into their late twenties and even early thirties, there are behaviors that you can choose to insure that your relationship is intentional, honest, and moving in the right direction.

It would be easy to look at the indicators of *heart marriage*—monogamy, cohabitation, early sexual involvement, and a prolonged relationship with growing reluctance to marry—and just say, "Don't do that!" Unfortunately, it is not that simple. The mysteries of attraction and sexuality, combined with the realities of economics, added to the freedom of mostly reliable birth control, require a more nuanced answer. Today many couples are searching for positive ways to approach these realities with the ultimate goal of a long lasting and satisfying legal marriage. Let's take a look at three couples who made deliberate decisions about their dating behavior that helped them avoid *heart marriage* and allowed them the time and boundaries to make the conscious choice to marry with clear hopes, goals, and aspirations.

Jennifer and Lance

Jennifer had been a thoughtful and introspective young girl and grew into a beautiful, contemplative young woman. She had a serious boyfriend in high school and while they kissed (a lot) and did some heavy petting (not much) they never had intercourse. This relationship ended when they both went to college. Jennifer was disillusioned at college by the casual sex she observed and by the way it seemed that women were judged only by external appearances. She found refuge in her faith and over the years began to think in terms of a lifelong commitment to celibacy. She met Lance at church at a young adult social event. The two had mutual friends who thought they would be perfect for each other. Lance was a reserved radiologist. He had dated many women but no one very seriously. He was interested in Jennifer but she was hard to read. After a month of small talk at church, Lance asked Jennifer for a date. She blushed deeply but gathered her courage to tell him what she would consider in terms of getting to know him.

Before meeting Lance, Jennifer had heard about the concept of "courting." Courting is a style of dating that involves the families of the couple in the decision-making process and in which the couple see one another only in group settings and where there is very little or no physical contact. After seeing many of her girlfriends hurt when their relationships became sexual quickly, Jennifer decided she wanted another way, if she dated at all. When she mentioned her interest in "courting" to her parents and sister, they were sure no man would ever go along with such an extreme proposition. However, they had not met Lance. At age 29, Lance was ready for a serious relationship that would hopefully lead to marriage. When Jennifer told him that she would like to get to know him using the "courting" model, he was intrigued. He liked it that she was taking their possible relationship so seriously and agreed to try out this new way. First, he had to meet with her parents and get to know them. Their insights and approval were then necessary before Jennifer and Lance could proceed. Jennifer's parents liked Lance immediately and sensed that he was a kind and sensitive fellow who would respect and understand their daughter. For the next few months, Jennifer and Lance got to know each other, but always in the company of mutual friends or family. Following the strict directives of courting, they did not have physical contact, even refraining from holding hands.

This time of getting to know one another while in a group setting gave both Jennifer and Lance the opportunity to see how each related to their families and friends. They both became comfortable with the other's family and there was a desire to proceed to the next level of courting. The next step was for Lance to have another direct conversation with Jennifer's parents where he would indicate his desire to know Jennifer better, hopefully become engaged, and then to marry Jennifer. In this style of courting, her parents would then discuss this proposal with Jennifer and if she agreed, they would proceed in the relationship toward an engagement.

Jennifer did feel that she loved Lance and through their shared activities had come to know him well. She believed they had many important things in common including their faith and commitment to family. While she definitely felt a physical attraction to Lance, seeing him in group settings kept the relationship from getting sexual. When the courting moved to the next level that indicated an interest in engagement and marriage, Jennifer and Lance revisited their earlier commitment to no physical contact. They decided that they would hold hands, and allow only a goodnight kiss and hug at the end of their evenings. They also decided that while they would go to dinner, movies, and other dates as a couple now, they would not spend time alone in their respective apartments. They reaffirmed their commitment to saving a sexually intimate relationship for marriage.

Jennifer and Lance married in a candlelight religious ceremony, surrounded by family and friends. It had been eighteen months from the beginning of the courting relationship to the wedding.

Jennifer and Lance present an extreme response to the current trend of early sexual involvement, cohabitation, and the heartbreak that can occur with multiple boyfriend or girlfriend relationships. While the courting model is too strident for most couples, it will surely prevent the occurrence of *heart marriage*. And although few choose this approach, courting is a very deliberate and intentional way of moving toward marriage that deeply involves the families of the couple. By using the courting model, Jennifer and Lance spent a lot of time talking and getting to know each other without relying on the closeness of sex to draw them together. Their willingness to involve their families in this process added a level of accountability for their actions that is often missing in romantic relationships. They were monogamous from the very beginning, as a part of the clearly verbalized courting plan. They did not come close to cohabiting, as they did not even spend time in each other's apartments unless other people were present. The relationship progressed and continued to deepen as they developed an emotional bond and committed friendship, which culminated with their marriage after eighteen months.

The practice of courting, which is reminiscent of an earlier time in history, seems to be making a comeback of sorts. In fact, there are books, blogs, and websites devoted to giving guidelines and support to this type of relationship. Some churches are heavily promoting courting as an alternative to serial dating and the pressure to become sexually intimate with one's current romantic interest. In all candor, courting is a measure that is too rigid for most people, but fortunately, it is not the only way to avoid *heart marriage*.

SHERITH AND BEN

Sherith was a feisty, headstrong, intelligent young woman. She excelled academically and was a talented artist, especially in drama and dance. She was not a classic beauty but with her love of life and extroverted personality, she had many admirers. For all her romantic prospects, though, she really was a one-man woman and had only three boyfriends by the age of twenty-five. The first two had been in high school and the third while in college. She had fallen totally in love with Keith in college. He was very much like her and the two could go toe-to-toe debating any subject and then spend the whole night dancing. He never pressed her sexually and they mostly just kissed. They talked about becoming physically intimate, but he wanted to take it slow and she admired his restraint. The pair began to talk about marriage happening after their respective college graduations. Sherith was totally devoted to Keith and began to think about a wedding. When Keith abruptly broke off the engagement, Sherith was devastated and had trouble understanding what had happened. She struggled to regain her footing and doubted her ability to judge people. She went to counseling for a while to help recover from the betrayal. (Much later it would be revealed that Keith was gay and was wrestling with his sexual identity during his college years.)

Sherith graduated from college with high honors and moved to another city for graduate school. She had no trouble attracting suitors, but now was unable to trust her judgment and quickly found reasons to not see anyone after a first or second date. She immersed herself in study groups and got involved in the community. She became a Big Sister to an inner city young girl who needed a friend and mentor, and eventually noticed Ben, who volunteered as a Big Brother. Ben was tall and lanky with unruly blond hair and kind eyes. They saw each other at meetings and their interactions were friendly. Sherith felt a definite attraction to Ben and he seemed interested in her and yet neither one pursued the other outside their volunteer work. Sherith told her girlfriends about Ben and they convinced her to ask him out. Their first "date" was for a cup of coffee. The two talked for three hours and realized they had many shared interests. Ben was a high school English teacher at an inner city school, an environmentalist, and a master gardener. Sherith had been committed to social justice issues and was excited when she realized Ben shared a commitment to some of those things as well.

Over the next six months, they had coffee occasionally and went hiking a couple of times. Sherith really liked Ben but couldn't tell about his level of interest. She finally decided to have a straightforward conversation with him and tell him she liked him and wanted to know if he saw their relationship as strictly a friendship or was there the possibility of a romance. Ben was thrilled by this direct conversation from such an interesting woman and said he was indeed interested in a romantic relationship. While this forthright conversation was scary to initiate for Sherith, it laid the groundwork for the start of an intentional, open friendship that would grow fairly quickly into a deep, committed love. Both Sherith and Ben had hoped for lifelong marriage and a partner who would share their desire to make the world a better place. Within six months, Ben wanted to talk about marriage, but Sherith realized she was still scarred from the earlier breakup with Keith. In keeping with their decision to be totally honest, she shared her fears with Ben. Ben affirmed his love and said he would wait until Sherith was ready. He also verbalized his intent to demonstrate through actions and words his promise to marry her when that day came. They enjoyed a physical relationship but did not have inter-course. They did have frank discussions about sex and what they wanted in a sexual partner. Both Sherith and Ben were virgins, and felt sexual expression was best within the confines of marriage. However, at their ages, twenty-five and thirty-one, respectively, they were both ready and wanted to have sex.

Ben proposed to Sherith and they began making wedding plans. Prior to the engagement, they had spent occasional nights together and had gone on overnight camping trips but had not had intercourse. One month prior to the wedding, they decided they were ready to have sex and did so. In a way, it resolved all the suspense and mystery as well as the lofty expectations often associated with honeymoon sex. They married in the early fall, in an outdoor ceremony that celebrated nature as well as their love and commitment. They had known each other for two years, but from the time of their first date to their wedding was twelve months.

Sherith and Ben are another example of a couple whose relationship pro-gressed in a forward manner, culminating in marriage, without falling prey to the uncertainty and hurt of a *heart marriage*. The hallmark of their partnership was an open, honest sharing of feelings, hopes, and dreams from the very start. Neither of them withheld past hurts or their expecta-tions for the future. They became monogamous as soon as they discussed dating one another exclusively. Although the two enjoyed kissing, holding hands, hugging, back rubs, foot massages, and other physically intimate and pleasurable activities, they refrained from sexual intercourse until one month prior to their wedding. When they did have sex, it did not "just happen" in the heat of the moment. They discussed their growing desire and decided the time was right even though their impending nuptials were a month off. While they spent occasional nights together, they did not live together. Finally, their relationship was never stagnant and they did not experience a prolonged engagement or any reluctance to marry.

Sherith and Ben present a much different model from that of Jennifer and Lance. However, one commonality of the two relationships is the very intentional nature of their communication with one another. Remember that *heart marriage* occurs not simply when couples practice the behaviors consistent with marriage over a long period of time, but when they do so without an intentional and articulated agreement to marry. In short, they are acting married, but haven't agreed to be married and often have not even discussed whether either person desires to be married. Being forthright about your values and expectations for relationships can be hard and exposes one's vulnerability, especially when a new friendship is in the early stages. In the long-term, though, this is the healthiest way to start and maintain all relationships whether they are strictly friendships or romantic partnerships. Because these two couples shared their expectations early, no one was under false illusions about where the other person was emotionally. They also spent time getting to know each other before starting an intimate physical relationship. They all knew they wanted a life that included marriage and desired to enter the marriage relationship with as much integrity and honesty as possible. Does this mean that Jennifer and Lance and Sherith and Ben will never have problems or conflict? Absolutely not. It does mean that they have set a precedent of relating to each other that will aid them when they encounter problems and issues that face all married couples at some time or another. Let's introduce one more couple who also avoided *heart marriage*, but their relationship looks much different from the ones just described.

Cristina and Tommy

Cristina was a passionate, somewhat insecure, but dedicated nursing student. Some people thought she looked like Snow White with her dark hair, ivory complexion, and crystal clear blue eyes. She was perceived somewhat as a dichotomy with her innocent good looks but she was fairly earthy in regards to life, a trait that found her well loved by her patients as she cared for them body and soul. It also made her attractive to men and she was one of those women who, even as a teenager, always had a boyfriend. While she wasn't promiscuous, she did enjoy sex and had intercourse with several boyfriends. Much to her dismay, Cristina had noticed that once a relationship turned sexual, her boyfriends seemed possessive and became focused mostly on the sex. At this point in her life she was reconsidering her casual attitude toward sex and had decided to try to refrain from early sexual involvement with any future boyfriends. She was in this mindset when she met Tommy.

Tommy was an intense young man and in his first year of law school when he met Cristina at a party. He couldn't help but notice that Cristina's quiet magnetism was attracting a lot of attention. For all his accomplishments, Tommy was fairly shy. He was so intrigued with this girl who looked like Snow White that he overcame his reticence and quickly asked her out when he noticed she was leaving the party. Cristina had already accepted another invitation and had to turn him down. She did offer her phone number and told him to call her. He called her the next day and the two decided on a date. They liked each other immediately and sensed a strong physical attraction. They did not discuss their sexual histories in detail but disclosed enough so both knew the other had had previous sexual relationships. Both enjoyed biking and jogging and studying together. Tommy pretty quickly was pushing for intercourse and Cristina wanted this too, but stood by her personal resolve to postpone sex until the relationship was further along. She didn't tell Tommy the reasons, only that she wanted to wait until she was sure. He didn't question what that meant to her, but accepted it at face value. They did enjoy some fun make-out sessions before having sex four months into the relationship. Cristina told Tommy she loved him at that point.

They continued to enjoy outdoor sports, and met and got to know their mutual families. They did spend some nights and weekends together, but each maintained an apartment. After being together for eighteen months, Tommy broached the subject of living together. By then Christina was working full time as a nurse and Tommy was in his final year of law school. Cristina hoped her answer wouldn't end the relationship when she told him she wanted more than to simply live together. Shortly after that Tommy asked Cristina to marry him. They were married in a simple traditional ceremony with about one hundred family members and friends as witnesses. From the time of their first date to the date of their wedding had been two years.

Cristina and Tommy present yet another example of a relationship that moved toward legal marriage in a timely way avoiding the pitfall of *heart marriage*. While they did have a sexual relationship, they delayed its onset as compared to previous relationships and did not become intimate before getting to know one another, at least somewhat. They did not have the deep disclosures that had marked the relationships of Jennifer and Lance or Sherith and Ben, but Cristina stuck with her resolve about early sex and when Tommy wanted to live together, Cristina was clear in saying she was looking for more in their future than cohabitation. Quite possibly, it was Cristina's clarity and her courage to act upon it along with Tommy's desire for a future with her that moved the relationship along, resulting in marriage after two years.

From these three examples, a number of straightforward behaviors can be pointed out that will help couples avoid becoming heart married. First, in terms of sex, the safest way to avoid *heart marriage* is to avoid sexual intimacy until marriage takes place. Statistics indicate that it is common today for couples to have sex before marriage and many of these couples go on to have fulfilling, happy marriages. However, if a couple chooses to have a sexual relationship and still wants to avoid *heart marriage*, sex should be delayed at least until the couple first gets to know each other on a nonphysical basis. This helps the couple avoid the unintentional binding of their hearts and insures a more purposeful relationship decision that is not clouded by the intensity of sexual intimacy. There is no magic timetable so each couple has to make that determination, but at the very least, several months without a sexual relationship allow a couple some time to determine whether they are compatible and likewise to expose areas of incompatibility that could be problematic.

Second, in terms of cohabitation, the best way to avoid *heart marriage* is to avoid living together. The occasional nights spent together are different from four or five nights a week. This is where couples often try to hedge their bets and tell themselves they are not living together because they are maintaining two residences. If you are spending most nights together, you are at risk for *heart marriage*. Currently, couples are moving toward cohabitation to save money. While it may make financial sense, we believe that if money is seen as the main consideration in relationship decisions, errors will result. The only exception to this is what is described as prenuptial cohabitation, when a couple moves into the same residence shortly before their already announced and planned wedding. The literature currently differentiates between cohabitation and prenuptial cohabitation. Again, unless the wedding is planned and the date set, couples deceive themselves by trying to characterize their living together as prenuptial.

Next, in terms of monogamy, it is an expectation in legal marriage and is a positive behavior in any serious relationship. The couple should discuss the decision to be monogamous and be clear that both participants are practicing monogamy if it is seen as a relationship that is moving toward marriage. The practice of monogamy alone will not result in *heart marriage.*

Finally, in terms of timing, couples in relationships that endure for many years without the clearly stated intention to marry are at risk of being heart married. While there are legitimate reasons to delay marriage such as finishing school, family concerns, or maturity issues, couples need to discern why a relationship is prolonged and not moving toward marriage. The familiarity that comes with long-term relationships combined with sex or cohabitation will lead to *heart marriage.* The passing of the years should be understood to have consequences for the couple, especially the woman in terms of her hopes for childbearing. There is no specific number of years that can be stated with authority, but when one member of the couple wants to be married and the other does not and they have been together for over two years, there are obviously issues that need to be resolved.

Avoiding *heart marriage* doesn't necessarily insure that your marriage will be a happy and fulfilling one, but it does allow you to make a clear, deliberate, and well thought out choice as to who and when you will marry. This chapter has discussed the most straightforward ways to prevent *heart marriage* from taking place, but for many of you, it already has. If that is the case, then the next two chapters will be particularly interesting. One will discuss the concept of *serial heart marriage* as a pattern of relationship behavior. It will consider how this pattern so easily happens, the dangers of the pattern, and the specific and detailed steps needed to break the cycle of *heart marriage.* The other will help you discern whether your *heart marriage* can transition into a committed legal marriage. For now, though, if you want to insure that your relationships do not become *heart marriages,* take the steps outlined below.

Taking It to Heart: A Call to Action

❤ Avoid having a sexual relationship until legally married. If you choose to have a sexual relationship, before doing so allow enough time early in the friendship to really get to know the person and whether their hopes and dreams are compatible with your own.

❤ Do not live together! Maintain separate living spaces, and if you must, spend only occasional nights together.

❤ If your relationship is serious—it has been in place for two years or more, and if you or your partner desire to be legally married but a marriage is not planned—immediately have an open and honest discussion about the future of the relationship.

❤ If after two or more years in your relationship you realize that you and your partner do not have the same goals and desires in regard to your future and marriage, stop wishing and break off the relationship!

10

Serial Heart Marriage

I Can't Believe I've Done It Again

MOST BEHAVIOR IS HABITUAL and relationship behavior is no exception. A habit, as we know, is difficult to break, whether it is biting
one's nails, overeating, using curse words, or running late. Certainly, it
is no surprise that "how one does relationships" can become a pattern
of behavior that repeats itself and is difficult to change. In fact, without
awareness, an intentional decision, a sound strategy, and accountability,
it is likely that, as with other habits, a relationship pattern such as *heart
marriage* will occur again and again. In chapter 9 we discussed the most
direct ways to avoid *heart marriage*, but obviously there are those of you
who have already experienced *heart marriage* and the pain that it causes.
You may have married as a result and are now divorced or you may have
wasted a number of years on a relationship that was never going anywhere. The question you may be asking yourself is whether this trend can
be reversed? Is the rather straightforward advice of the previous chapter
realistic once you have an established pattern of dating behavior that involves dating the same person for long periods of time, sexual intimacy,
and some form of cohabiting? Are you destined to become heart married
over and over again?

MORE ABOUT RANDY AND MARTHA SUE

Randy and Martha Sue were the couple in chapter 8 who began dating
in college, continued through pharmacy school, started their practice,
bought and moved into a house together, and continued this relationship

for about seven years before an excruciating split. The breakup occurred after Martha Sue was unfaithful, but the signs of *heart marriage* as well as indicators of the need for a *heart divorce* were obvious, though unnoticed before that. After much heartache on Randy's part, he began to "come around" and act like himself again, only to begin a relationship with another pharmacist, Diane, who practiced in his group. In very short order, they were monogamous, sexually active, and though not cohabiting, spent most nights together with Randy keeping clothes and toothbrush at Diane's place. Randy had done it again, his heart was married, or well on its way, and he was once again devastated when Diane, after about six months, abruptly ended the relationship.

In the case of *heart marriage*, the habitual pattern involves becoming monogamous and sexually active early in a relationship, slipping into a pattern of cohabiting or spending most nights together, and most important, doing this without an intentional decision that includes serious discussion about the desire for a committed relationship or plans for the future. Basically, boy meets girl, they are attracted to each other, there is strong chemistry, and they talk in general about their dreams. But, thinking it is too soon, they do not specifically talk about their desire for a committed relationship. They connect and appear to enjoy and understand each other; and . . . it just happens. Without realizing it, the couple is together six months, then a year, then six months more, and their hearts are as married as they were in their previous relationship. When this phenomenon occurs a second and third time, we call it *serial heart marriage* and it is dangerous and dreadfully painful. Moreover, because *heart marriage*, by definition, is a prolonged relationship with no formal commitment to the future, it is a waste of time. This energy could be spent on developing a relationship with a partner who has the same desire for a committed marriage, increasing the possibility for a full and satisfying life. The assault to an individual's self-esteem and belief in relationships, in general, can have a long-term negative effect on individuals who find themselves in *serial heart marriages*. One *heart marriage* is painful enough, whether it leads to a marriage that ends in a divorce or more constructively ends with a *heart divorce*, saving a couple from the strain and hurt of a failed marriage. Two or more *heart marriages* can leave individuals so broken that it is difficult for them to recover and form a healthy, happy, and satisfying relationship. In fact, in chapter 5, the discussion of cohabitation, one of the elements of *heart marriage*, notes that serial cohabiters have a higher incidence of divorce than those who either do not cohabit or do so only once.

It is reasonable then to ask how such a destructive relationship pattern can be so easily repeated, especially since it almost always causes distress to the participants. The answer to that question is more complex than it may seem. First and foremost, the answer lies in the fact that many couples simply do not name and clearly articulate the fact that they have been heart married, nor do they look at the behavioral decisions they made which promote *heart marriage*. They often just tell themselves that they were stupid, overlooked obvious signs, and won't let that happen again. Frequently they focus on having selected the wrong person, rather than the behavioral choices that they made in the relationship. This book began by quoting Woody Allen when he said, "The heart wants what the heart wants," (Isaacson, "The Heart," last paragraph) and indeed it does, unless one invites reason and intentionality into decisions of the heart.

The truth is that the cultural environment today creates a ripe landscape for *heart marriage* and that doesn't change for a person from relationship to relationship. Often young men and women are delaying marriage, yet love is depicted in the media as synonymous with sexual intimacy and cohabitation. It isn't unusual to see couples on primetime television living together and becoming pregnant outside of marriage. Getting married often appears to be an afterthought. This is not to say that this phenomenon is glorified, but it is certainly normalized. Unfortunately, the destiny of these "after thought" marriages is not as often the subject of the sitcoms.

Monogamy, in itself, is a positive practice and one that is still the most accepted in romantic relationships and marriage. Legally, monogamy is the expectation in marital relationships in our society and that expectation also appears to hold true for dating relationships. Being involved with one person at a time is simply easier, less hassle, and usually all that folks have the emotional energy for. It also is natural for individuals who care about each other to desire to be together sexually, physically, and emotionally. They long to spend time together, go to bed and wake up with each other, and share dreams together. Once individuals have been in an intimate sexual relationship, it often becomes more acceptable to them to cross that line and follow their normal and natural desires to be sexually intimate each time they enter a new relationship. Monogamy with sexual intimacy and cohabitation are elements of *heart marriage* and promote its occurrence. Because couples tend to repeat these patterns of behavior, they find themselves in *serial heart marriages*.

The first *heart marriage* typically occurs with couples when they are fairly young, yet the elements of *heart marriage* seem perhaps even more natural once couples grow older and have additional relationships. Again, since *heart marriage* is by definition a prolonged relationship, often followed by a marriage that fails, a person is usually in the late twenties or thirties when *serial heart marriage* comes into play. With couples at that age, it is more likely that their contemporaries are married and raising families, instead of dating and still shopping around for the perfect person. It seems even more normal for older couples to settle down in what looks like marriage, even if they don't make it legal. They typically follow what appears to be the natural progression of a relationship—the couple meets, becomes sexually intimate and practically cohabits. This has been their behavior with partners in the past and the pattern becomes a habit that is hard to break without intentionally setting boundaries.

Even after a failed relationship, and perhaps especially after a bad relationship, the heart seems to yearn for love and closeness and often one's greatest desire is to prove that same kind of "true love" that has been imagined and daydreamed about is really possible. Individuals become, in a way, desperate, for the right relationship. Frequently women begin to feel the real urge to have children and look at their time as running out. Although ultimately counterproductive, they want badly to create a serious relationship and hope that it will lead to marriage.

The bottom line with how *serial heart marriages* come about, even in light of previous painful experiences, is that behavior is habitual; and common relationship behavior in this society, especially with couples who are getting older, mimics the elements of marriage in many ways. Unless one recognizes that *heart marriage* is the cause of the situation, it will recur. To prevent *serial heart marriage*, behavioral boundaries must be set and strategies put into place that encourage healthier relationship decisions.

So what is it about *heart marriage* that one needs to be aware of in order to establish healthy boundaries and establish new behavior patterns? We have discussed the elements of *heart marriages*—monogamy, sexual intimacy, cohabitation, and the reluctance to marry over time. Should the couple choose a different path to defend themselves from *heart marriage* or *serial heart marriage*? Certainly, it is possible to establish boundaries around sexual intimacy and cohabitation in a relationship. Having been there before, a couple can simply choose to eliminate those two behaviors from any future relationships, or at least delay them. The question may arise, however, of how long a couple should wait. Also, we do know that there are certainly couples who marry happily, who were sexually intimate prior to their marriage and who cohabited. Studies about cohabitation tend to differentiate prenuptial cohabitation from cohabitation in general and define it as living together for a finite period of time prior to a determined wedding date. This would be the case of the engaged couple who has a wedding date set; is in the midst of wedding plans; and who for convenience, finances, or simply because they have the desire, go ahead and move in together before the actual wedding day. As yet, there is no evidence that prenuptial cohabitation increases the possibility of divorce. (Sloan, "Cohabitation," 106–113) It should be noted here, however, that the couple who is intentional about marriage and making plans for a wedding within a reasonable amount of time as the natural progression of a serious relationship, may indeed have hearts that are filled with love and adoration, but by our definition, are not heart married. Rather they are in a relationship with an intentional and articulated commitment to a future together. They are, in fact, an engaged couple.

Inasmuch as monogamy is always present in *heart marriage*, you might ask whether one should "swear off" of monogamous relationships in order to safeguard against *heart marriage*. That seems an unreasonable and unlikely strategy. There is certainly not anything wrong with monogamy, especially once a relationship is clearly serious, but cutting off all possibilities of dating or meeting other people too quickly in a relationship should be avoided. Also, if the decision to be monogamous is made, it should be purposeful and agreed upon between the couple with a clear understanding of their rationale for such a decision.

Finally, how long should a relationship last before reluctance to marry becomes a real red flag? One could argue that the desire to marry early in a relationship could also be looked at skeptically. Unfortunately, there is no magic formula that specifies the exact amount of time it takes to make a constructive decision to marry. If marriage is one's ultimate goal, however, it should be stated clearly and openly in the relationship.

The remainder of this chapter will be dedicated to three simple guidelines to help couples avoid *serial heart marriage*. It should be noted that if the reader hasn't yet experienced *heart marriage*, the same advice can help one avoid *heart marriage* altogether.

Guideline 1: Be intentional in your relationship decision-making and open in communicating your ultimate relationship goals.

Understand that the key differentiating factor in *heart marriage* that transcends all other elements is the lack of intentionality. Remember that *heart marriage* just seems to happen over time. Couples may talk casually early in the relationship about the future, but practice binding behaviors such as sexual intimacy and cohabitation before engaging in any frank conversations about what they want in a lasting relationship. If the future is discussed, it is too late to make rational decisions because of the emotional involvement. Other times, the couple has often been so noncommittal in this regard that if one partner later wants to discuss the future, there is hesitancy fearing that the discussion will result in an argument or in "running off" the other partner. The most important thing to remember if you have already been involved in a *heart marriage* once is to approach any new relationship with intentionality and be aware and in charge of your decisions. Being in charge of your decisions and knowing what your goals are in a relationship, identifying honestly the probable outcomes of behavior based on experience, assessing the pros and cons before acting, and then choosing the path that best gets you to your goals is a sound recipe for avoiding *heart marriage* once or multiple times. Finally, being intentional means taking full responsibility for your decisions and monitoring the results, so that you are aware of the need for a different course of action if necessary before too much time has passed. Following this suggestion will transform your relationships from happenstance to purposeful and will be an important first step toward creating a healthy environment for your relationships. At the same time, it will help insure that the heart doesn't marry without your knowing it.

Guideline 2: Set boundaries for yourself; articulate them clearly and communicate them to your partner.

Having been involved previously in *heart marriage* and therefore having gained valuable insight into the contributing factors, it is important to set boundaries around the four basic elements we have discussed. In order for boundaries to be useful, the individual who is setting them must be very clear and comfortable with what they are. Once clear, the individual must be prepared to articulate them with confidence to his/her relationship partner at the appropriate time. Ideally, that discussion should take place on the front end of the relationship before a boundary is being pushed. It also will likely be necessary to revisit the boundaries throughout the course of the relationship.

In regard to sexual intimacy, you must remind yourself of its power to bind a couple together. Not only does sex create an emotional involvement, it also results in the emission of oxytocins, which have been proven to bind the couple and create a feeling of closeness based simply on the sexual engagement and not on any rational decisions around whether the person shares the same values, goals, and ambitions. Given this knowledge, it is wise to set clear boundaries for yourself as to whether you will choose to become involved sexually in your relationships. More and more couples are deciding to delay sexual intimacy until marriage as evidenced by the number of college abstinence clubs that have begun to spring up, not only in the Bible belt, but also in very elite colleges that are considered to be liberal institutions such as Harvard, M.I.T., and Princeton. (Aviv, "On a Date With," 31) Young people in these growing abstinence societies cite such reasons as showing respect for each other, practicing self-discipline, and maintaining one's dignity. They seem to understand the emotional connection that occurs when couples have sex and recognize that bonding as premature and a barrier to developing a healthy relationship. Even in this modern era, abstinence is a viable choice and it appears the pendulum may be swinging in that direction, even if ever so slightly. Reasons for this shift include, yet go beyond, religious doctrine and beliefs. Some embrace the wisdom of honoring the dignity of one's body and viewing the uniquely intimate sexual relationship as one that is reserved wisely for one's lifelong mate.

Even so, you may see sexual intimacy as inevitable as a relationship progresses over time, however that does not negate the need for clear boundaries. In that case, the boundary should include an understanding of what is too quick in a relationship for sexual intimacy such that it creates an unhealthy closeness and gets ahead of rational decision-making. If you feel that sexual intimacy would enhance your healthy and purposeful relationship, moving to that new level of closeness should be discussed to ascertain if you are both at the same place and what it will mean to the two of you. At the very least, a frank discussion around this issue increases the possibility that decisions are intentional. And a discussion of birth control methods and sexually transmitted diseases is an absolute necessity.

Monogamy is the preference for most couples, but in order to avoid *serial heart marriage* it is wise to create a boundary that allows you some space and time before making an intentional decision to be monogamous in a dating relationship. You may be thinking that often once a couple begins to date, the opportunities for dating others appear to disappear. We would contend that this absence of opportunity more accurately occurs because of behavioral decisions made by individuals, such as spending all their time together, abandoning going out with friends, and no longer going to events and activities alone. They are simply not open to seeing other people and send that message when in the company of the opposite sex. None of this is inherently bad, but it is important not to get into that trap too early in a relationship. It is much healthier to become monogamous only after you have verbally articulated the decision to do so based on a rationale that includes similar goals for the future of your relationship. In short, be intentional and purposeful in this choice. Don't just fall into monogamy or assume that your partner feels the same way you do.

Similarly, making a purposeful decision around cohabitation prior to being confronted with the temptation is important in avoiding *serial heart marriage*. Because cohabitation often evolves before the outright "moving in together" occurs, a serious and open discussion about your past experience and your thoughts about cohabitation should happen fairly early in a new relationship, especially if there appears to be a substantial interest in each other. Such a discussion should be met with respect and a commitment to abide by your decision. Though there is very little conclusive evidence about the effect of cohabitation on the outcome of a marriage, there doesn't appear to be any evidence that it has a discernible positive effect. Studies do indicate, however, that cohabitation rarely results in a permanent union with 50 percent of such relationships ending within one year and 90 percent within five years. (Sloan, "Cohabitation," 106–113) These statistics along with your experience with a previous *heart marriage* should be enough to inform your decision on this issue. The safest course is to choose not to cohabit and to maintain your own space and privacy, not just by having two residences, but also by enforcing privacy and time boundaries such that you aren't spending all of your nights and available daytime hours together. You may, however, decide that you will consider cohabitation if there are obvious signs of a forthcoming marriage. This is dangerous territory where *heart marriage* is concerned and ideally discouraged, but certainly until wedding plans are announced and a date is set. Whatever the decision, open discussion around your desire for a committed and lasting relationship, clear guidelines for how long you will cohabit before marriage, and the determination to act if your partner does not honor these guidelines is a sound course of action. This intentional approach is necessary to prevent *serial heart marriage*.

Finally, it is important to set boundaries around the inability to marry over time. After having been heart married previously and experiencing the pain and real consequences of wasted time in a relationship doomed to failure, it is important to be clear on the front end about your ultimate relationship goals. It is also helpful to have in mind a timeline for assessing the progress of the relationship. Understanding that relationships develop at different paces, the timeline may consist of milestone checkpoints rather than a hard deadline. For instance, you could decide to designate a time at six months and perhaps a year when you and your partner will assess the relationship in regard to your ultimate goals. After a year, if the relationship isn't making the kind of progress that is clear and evident, make the hard decision to change course and move on before you find yourself stuck in another prolonged relationship with no real plans for the future you desire.

Guideline 3: Hold yourself accountable for maintaining boundaries and assessing the relationship against your goals.

Finally, boundaries are of no use unless they are maintained. This is your responsibility, not your partner's. While it may be your partner's responsibility in a healthy relationship to respect your boundaries, you are in charge of your own destiny. Maintaining those boundaries allows them to accomplish what they are meant to accomplish which is to avoid another *heart marriage*. You must also be dedicated to maintaining open discussion with your partner and assessing your relationship using your ultimate goals as a yardstick for success. If after your assessment, the relationship doesn't measure up favorably to your goals, then it is your responsibility and obligation to yourself to act accordingly and change course without delay.

Being intentional in your relationship decision-making and communicating openly your ultimate goals, setting and articulating clear boundaries, holding yourself accountable to those boundaries, and assessing the progress of your relationship against your goals will not insure the success of all future relationships, but it will help you avoid *heart marriage* and emotional paralysis. We know that all initial attractions, no matter how strong, do not develop into lasting relationships. The truth is, however, that relationships that are based on thoughtful decision-making, clear boundaries, accountability, and reasoned assessment have a much greater chance of developing into successful and healthy partnerships. The important message in this chapter is that *serial heart marriage* compounds already frayed emotions, wastes precious time, and often affects an individual's self-esteem, attitudes about relationships, and ability to trust and form lasting partnerships. By following these suggestions, you will avoid *heart marriage* that binds you in a destructive way by virtue of its lack of intentionality. Most important, these guidelines can prevent you from going down a path to a marriage that has little chance of survival or from getting stuck in a prolonged relationship that ends in divorce. The great cost that is paid in heartache, wasted time, and missed opportunity can be avoided.

After so much discussion about *heart marriage*, you may be asking the question, "Aren't all couples in love heart married and do all *heart marriages* end badly?" Such frequently asked questions and others will be addressed later in this book. In the next chapter, we will talk about our observations regarding *heart marriages* that can and do transition into lasting relationships and how that happens.

Taking It to Heart: A Call to Action

❧   Make a list of the behaviors you practice habitually that have led to *heart marriage*.

❧   If you are truly interested in breaking the cycle of *serial heart marriage*, set clear boundaries that eliminate sexual intimacy and cohabitation.

❧   If you are in a relationship, discuss your boundaries with your girl/boyfriend. It's not too late. If the person respects you, he/she will respect them. If not, break off the relationship now.

❧   Establish these new boundaries early in any future relationship and enforce them with a vengeance.

11

Making Heart Marriage Work

Can a Heart Marriage Transition
into a Lasting Legal Marriage?

B Y NOW YOU ARE likely wondering, "Aren't all couples who are in love and have been together for a prolonged period, heart married?" And, "Haven't the hearts of most engaged couples become bound together?" These are legitimate questions and the answers are not simple. Surely, when a couple has been together for a considerable amount of time, they are significantly connected. The same is true of the committed couple in the midst of wedding plans. In fact, it is typical and desirable that engaged couples are intricately entwined and already joined together emotionally in an important way. Such a feeling is one of deep and abiding love based on shared decision-making that includes plans for the future and openly shared hopes and dreams. It is love that is reasonable as well as emotional. This is not the same concept, however, as what we refer to throughout this book as *heart marriage*.

In contrast, we have defined *heart marriage* as a relationship in which the couple has not openly and mutually stated their desire and plans for marriage and yet they behave as if they are married. In fact, emotionally they feel as married as if they had walked down the aisle and repeated their vows. Because of this, they often reach the point that they see no other alternative except marriage, while at the same time, they have great difficulty taking that step. This sense of resignation about the inevitability of their marriage is often felt in the face of many danger signals. Yet, for many couples, it is only when they finally take that step to legally confirm their union, that they are able to confront their real issues and entertain the idea of severing what they know is an unhealthy relationship.

It would be wrong, however, not to acknowledge that some *heart marriages* succeed. They do not always end in ill-advised marriage and a predictable divorce or result in wasted years in a relationship that ends with heartache and an unfulfilled future. There are indeed some couples who fit the profile of a *heart marriage* and yet do make the commitment and do transition into a lasting relationship. They get married and enjoy a rich and fulfilling married life.

Marilyn and Jonathan

Marilyn and Jonathan were the typical well-educated "twenty-something" couple. They met after college when their paths crossed among mutual friends. Both had serious relationships while in college that ended with the couples going their separate ways for job offers in different cities. They stayed in touch with their college loves for awhile, but the long distance relationships just didn't work out. Sensibly, both Marilyn and Jonathan decided that they would be open to meeting new people, and when they met each other, they clicked immediately. The two liked everything about each other. Not only were they physically attracted, but they also seemed to share the same goals, enjoy the same things, and come from similar backgrounds. Both grew up in Tennessee, lived in good neighborhoods, were active in their sororities and fraternities, were adored by their parents, and didn't appear to carry a lot of personal baggage.

Their relationship took off and they very quickly became sexually intimate and monogamous. They had separate apartments, but started to spend a great deal of time together. Sleeping over on the weekend was a pretty normal occurrence although they were committed to maintaining separate residences. Neither wanted the issue of a major move if the relationship ended and each enjoyed maintaining that bit of independence. They spoke very little of marriage, particularly in the beginning, except to agree that neither had been ready for marriage in college and they were perfectly happy being single at the present time. When months passed and then a year and they were still together, their friends and families began to anticipate that marriage might be in the picture. When asked if there might soon be an engagement ring, they typically laughed it off avoiding the question, but admitted that they did deeply care for each other.

Into the second year, things began to change for Marilyn and she started to think about marriage and was convinced that Jonathan was the kind of man she could spend the rest of her life with. Venturing to mention this, however, it became apparent that Jonathan was very cautious and pushed back on the subject. Although Marilyn and Jonathan came from divorced families, they maintained good relationships with their parents. In both cases, their parents had remarried and yet had remained cooperative with each other and were reasonably cordial. Both Marilyn and Jonathan were committed to making their marriage last and wanted to be sure before they selected a mate and married. It seemed, however, that Jonathan had been affected in ways that he had not realized. When it came to marriage, he just couldn't get comfortable. He wanted to be completely secure financially, absolutely certain that he was through with his single life, and dead certain that the marriage would be forever. He expressed this to Marilyn and she agreed, but knew that she was already there. She decided to be patient and give Jonathan time. After six months of silence on the subject, she sensed that their being in different spots emotionally was taking its toll and creating tension. She knew she needed to stand her ground and let Jonathan know how she was feeling.

Although they didn't realize it, Marilyn and Jonathan had become heart married. They loved each other, acted like a married couple, and hated the thought of breaking up. Instead of coming closer to marriage, however, Jonathan drew away even more. He just couldn't take that step. He was emotionally stuck with no sign of budging.

After many tears and much grief, they decided together that it would be best to break up. This lasted for a number of months during which they made half-hearted attempts to date other people. They were so miserable and no one else measured up, so they resumed their relationship. Marilyn was clear and open about her ultimate desire to marry, but decided that she would rather date Jonathan and not be married than be with anyone else. They resumed their sexual relationship, were monogamous, and again began spending nights together on weekends. Unfortunately, the reluctance to marry on Jonathan's part also remained the same. They broke up two more times before Marilyn made it clear to Jonathan not to call her again until he was ready to get married. She knew what she wanted, and even though Jonathan repeatedly claimed to love her and want her to be his wife, he just couldn't take the final step.

Almost a year later, Jonathan had become a partner in a thriving business. He had secured his financial future, spent plenty of time going out with friends and occasionally dating, and most important, had done a considerable amount of soul-searching. He knew that the only thing standing between him and a future with Marilyn was his fear and doubts about marriage in general. He came to realize that his past had caused him to be more than cautious; it had paralyzed him. He thought that his parents would be together forever, and yet their marriage had failed, so who was he to think he could do any better. When he confronted those doubts and fears, he realized that although there were no guarantees, he was in love with Marilyn. He did not have to make the same mistakes as his parents and was committed to making his marriage last. He felt confident that he would do the very best that he could to make that happen. His biggest fear now was that Marilyn would not have him back.

Marilyn had returned to graduate school and was now dating Martin, a personable and ambitious young dentist. She cared about him and thought that she would finally be able to bring closure to her feelings for Jonathan and move forward. When Jonathan called, she was hesitant and did not respond positively at first. Eventually, Jonathan's persistence and sincerity paid off and Marilyn ended her relationship with Martin. She and Jonathan began dating again and when Marilyn became truly convinced that he had confronted his doubt and was ready for marriage, she accepted an engagement ring and they began to plan their wedding. Although they had never cohabited before, with the wedding plans in progress, they bought a house together and attended premarriage counseling. Four years after their first date, they had a beautiful wedding and though still newly married, they continue to feel comfortable about their future together.

CONDITIONS CONDUCIVE TO A POSITIVE TRANSITION

Just as there are signs that indicate a relationship has become a *heart marriage* and signs that a *heart divorce* may be warranted, there are also several conditions that make it more likely that a *heart marriage* can transition into a lasting relationship. You will notice that all three conditions were present in the relationship just described between Marilyn and Jonathan.

Condition 1: The clearly articulated desire of one partner for a long-term commitment, usually marriage.

As has already been mentioned, statistics indicate that most individuals even in today's post-sexual revolution environment want to be married. Although anecdotally this may be more often the case with females, most men also express the desire to marry and have a family at some point in their lives. One of the signs of *heart marriage* is the reluctance to marry over time. Usually both parties have talked about marriage at one time or another, particularly early in the relationship, but the conversation is often in vague terms and always in the future. The conversation is an outgrowth of the high emotionalism of the early stages of love and takes on the same idealism with grandiose plans. As time goes on, there seem to be many reasons to postpone marriage and the couple may quit discussing it altogether. They sometimes begin to think and even verbally comment that because everything is fine as it is, there is really no good reason to marry. The couple becomes stuck and the relationship grows stagnant.

In order for a *heart marriage* to make the transition into a lasting, lifetime relationship, one of the partners must honestly and clearly articulate the desire for such a change. This declaration can result in conflict and even a breakup, but it is necessary for one person to break the existing pattern and confront the dissatisfaction he or she is feeling with the "going nowhere" status of the relationship. This admission establishes an environment of honesty where both individuals can become openly accountable for their feelings and actions. Only then, can purposeful decisions be made and forward movement take place.

Condition 2: A never wavering love and respect for each other, even in the face of doubts about marriage.

Heart marriage over time often becomes a war between the emotions and the mind. There is the strong feeling of love, but there are many signals that the relationship is not right. Along with those signals come doubts, creating tension and friction between the couple. The classic signs of the need for *heart divorce* arise in frequent quarrels, thoughts of leaving, the sense that one cannot plan for the future, and a general feeling of unease and foreboding. In short, although the couple may say they love each other and may indeed feel affection, passion, and caring for each other, there are many moments of doubt about their feelings. In fact, even when the heart married couple decides to go ahead and marry, these doubts typically do not go away. They experience alternating feelings of excitement and nagging hesitation. Unfortunately, they push the underlying feelings aside and plunge ahead.

Conversely, in situations where *heart marriage* eventually does make the successful transition into marriage, the one thing the couple remains sure of is their love and respect for each other. This appears to be the case both for the one who is unready for the final commitment of marriage as well as for the one who has articulated the desire to move the relationship forward. As *heart marriage* has been defined, there is a reluctance to marry, but the reluctance present in a successful transition scenario appears unrelated to the partner or incompatibility. Reluctance in this case rather centers on personal unreadiness resulting from doubts, fears, finances, or perhaps unmet goals. One or both of the parties are simply not ready to enter into marriage; however, they maintain the conviction that they are right for each other. Unlike other *heart marriages*, frequent arguments and unresolved issues are usually not present, except perhaps the unresolved issue of when to make the relationship a legal and binding one by marrying. Often, in fact, the person who is simply not ready is truly sorry and grieves for the pain it causes the other, desperately hoping that it doesn't result in the end of the relationship. Nevertheless, the individual is not willing to make the decision to marry simply to avoid the pain. In these cases, the refusal to marry is a difficult but mature decision that in the long run has the best interest of each other and the relationship at its core.

Condition 3: The willingness of the individual with the stated desire to marry to take personal responsibility and act individually to make a change regardless of the consequences; or, conversely, to remain patient and stay in the relationship with a renewed commitment to emotional honesty.

Sliding along with no honestly expressed desire for the future is most often the way the heart married couple exists. No one is talking about it, and no one is taking a stand. A critical condition, as earlier discussed, under which it appears that *heart marriage* can successfully transition into a lifelong commitment to marriage is that at least one person in the partnership has begun to talk about marriage as a desired goal. The third condition that makes the transition even more likely is that the person with the desired goal takes full responsibility for that desire and has the courage to act independently to make a change.

Usually taking action means to terminate the relationship if the other partner remains unable or unwilling to take that step. This action is different from issuing an ultimatum inasmuch as it is simply an independent decision to act while respecting the partner's right to decide to leave things as they are. While there may have been tears and arguments in the past over the subject, at this point the decision, while extremely sad to both partners, is one of determination and resignation that there is a difference in intention at the present time that can no longer be tolerated. The partner who is "stuck" typically continues to profess love for the other and the future desire to marry, but there is no action and no sign of any real movement. There may be concrete reasons that the person is unready, such as specific goals that he or she wishes to accomplish or an underlying emotional fear or dread that remains a stumbling block to marriage. The bottom line, however, is that one partner will not move forward to the next logical step in the relationship. Termination of the relationship with this level of maturity and honesty maintains respect for each other and does not focus on recrimination and blame. Because of that, the relationship is not permanently damaged, making it possible in the future to be resumed, if the unwilling partner becomes ready to make the marriage commitment. It is important, however, that when the relationship ends, the terminating partner makes a firm decision to move forward, establish new and healthy relationships, and pursue future goals. Even with that determination, there are times when the heart remains married and an individual is emotionally available if the original partner demonstrates authentic change, accompanied by concrete steps toward marriage.

Taking responsibility and acting independently, however, can also mean remaining in the relationship with a new level of emotional honesty. That is to acknowledge the desire to marry; to articulate it with unwavering resolve to the partner; and at the same time, to consciously make the decision to wait for the other individual to change course. This is equally as difficult as terminating the relationship because it requires a balance between the commitment to unending honesty and, at the same time, the determination to avoid nagging or attempting to push the partner to agree to marriage. When this is the action that is taken, the individual openly faces and accepts that one's partner is not ready to marry, even though it is painful to do so. There is always the risk that waiting may be unfruitful and ultimately a waste of valuable time. The decision to be patient and wait is most often made when there is a profound trust that the couple shares a deep love for one another and that the desire to marry will happen, albeit in the future. While it may appear that this latter course of action is more of the same, it is not. Rather it is an openly honest and conscious decision to trust the strength of the relationship and to give one's partner the time necessary to take concrete steps to marry. No longer is the desire unspoken or argued over, making it more likely that the relationship is not harmed irrevocably and increasing the chance that the time may come when the *heart marriage* will transition into a lasting, committed marriage.

CELESTE AND SCOTT

Celeste and Scott started dating their second year in college. They were a great looking couple and experienced a typical college romance, enjoying each other and having fun at fraternity parties, ballgames, and weekend excursions. Celeste had plans for a career as a physical therapist, but also hoped to marry and have children. Scott had dreams of playing tennis professionally. He was the number one player on his collegiate tennis team and everyone had high hopes for him. Celeste was supportive and liked the celebrity effect of dating a star athlete. All seemed to go well until graduation. Celeste expected that there would be talk of marriage and hinted about it, but Scott had no such plans. He was crazy about Celeste, but was focused on his tennis career. Unfortunately, he sustained an injury that kept him off the court, and he threw all of his energy into rehabilitation. Celeste's fear of college ending without a proposal began to create tension and Scott responded by cheating on her. They had been monogamous for three years and were sexually intimate. This was a big step for Celeste, because she truly believed that sexual intimacy was ideally reserved for marriage and certainly only to be shared with someone you love deeply. Their relationship began to feel too much like marriage to Scott and his indiscretion was an act of rebellion. When Celeste learned that Scott had been unfaithful right before graduation, she felt devastated, broke up with him, and started physical therapy training. Her heart was broken, but she continued her studies, while Scott played around. After about six months, Scott realized that he had messed up. He knew that he loved Celeste, but her desire for marriage had gotten the best of him. He wanted desperately to resume his relationship with Celeste and began to court her vigorously to win her back. By this time, Celeste had an apartment and was well on her way to her career. She still loved Scott, however, and a career was secondary to her desire to eventually marry and have a family. After several months she relented and she and Scott began to see each other again, virtually picking up where they left off.

For the next seven years, they were together exclusively. Out of respect for their parents and their own belief that cohabitation was not wise nor what they wanted to do, they kept separate residences. They did, however, continue to spend some nights together from time to time. One by one, Celeste's friends began to marry and each time she would be wistful and hint to Scott that perhaps it was time for them. In the meantime, Scott had tried unsuccessfully to break into the professional tennis circuit. As good as he was, he just couldn't quite make it. Since that was all he ever wanted to do, he floundered for awhile, trying to decide upon a career. He had a degree but no real direction, so spent a great deal of time playing tennis at the country club and winning amateur tournaments, keeping his dream alive. He did land a good sales job in pharmaceuticals and began to do well, but still wasn't ready to settle down. Scott loved Celeste, but he knew that once he married, there would be children and then his ability to continue to pursue his dreams and hang out with the guys would end.

Celeste became more and more anxious and moody. She had thought that once Scott got a job that he would put his dream of professional tennis aside and begin to think about the future with her that he had professed to eventually want. Each time Christmas or a birthday came around, she hoped for an engagement ring that didn't come. She loved Scott's family, but it was increasingly difficult for her to be with them. Scott's younger brother had married and she began to feel like an outsider. Scott's family loved Celeste but because there was no movement toward marriage, they began to wonder if this was the right person for their son. They thought that surely if he loved her, he would ask her to marry him. They spoke to him about it, and he maintained that he did adore Celeste, but he was simply not ready to marry. Celeste's mother also began to think the relationship was a dead end and counseled Celeste to break it off. Celeste was a beautiful young woman and would surely meet someone eager to settle down and have the family with her that she wanted so badly. Although Celeste considered her mother's advice seriously, she just couldn't do it.

Without a doubt, Celeste had become heart married and breaking up would feel like a painful divorce.

The truth is that Scott was also heart married, as evidenced by his inability to break up with Celeste even though he was in a stuck position when it came to marriage. Periodically, he thought about going ahead and getting the ring and proposing, but each time he simply couldn't do it. Scott knew he was making Celeste miserable even though that wasn't his intention. Many of his friends told him that ending the relationship would be the kindest thing he could do for Celeste, but he couldn't imagine being without her. He had already tried that and knew that when it came time for marriage, Celeste was the right girl. Even with his reluctance, Scott had a strong desire to have a family and valued family relationships. He knew that for him marriage was forever and his unwillingness to take that final step was not about his love for Celeste, rather it was an underlying determination to be sure that when his wedding day came, he was ready to be a good husband and father.

Finally, after many tears, talks, and ultimatums, Celeste made a decision. She knew what she wanted and had expressed it clearly to Scott. He continued to tell her that he loved her and that marriage was in the future. Even though others thought she was crazy, Celeste believed him. Celeste realized that she had to take responsibility for her behavior and for her decisions. She was choosing to stay in the relationship and watch all of her friends marry. He was not putting pressure on her to stay except to tell her that he loved her and there was no one else for him. In fact, he had expressed many times that he wouldn't blame her if she left him, but he couldn't marry her until he was ready. Coming to grips with the fact that she was making herself miserable, blaming Scott and filling herself with resentment, she knew it was time to make a change. For her, the change was to acknowledge her desire for marriage and to take one day at a time. She decided that she would no longer coax or beg or present ultimatums to Scott. She would enjoy each day with him and accept where he was. When she could do that no longer, she would make the decision to leave, but until then, she would trust that their love would eventually result in what they both said they wanted—marriage and children.

Although it was difficult, Celeste's resentment began to dissipate and the tension between them lessened. It wasn't perfect, but she no longer blamed Scott for her situation. Scott felt the change and was relieved. He began to prosper financially in his job and realized that he was a gifted salesman and that he enjoyed it. He could play tennis on the weekends, enter amateur tournaments, and feel good about that. Finally, when Celeste wasn't expecting it, Scott asked her to marry him and gave her a beautiful engagement ring. It had been a ten-year romance that everyone else had given up on, except Celeste and Scott.

The two were married in a conventional ceremony with a large wedding party. Celeste had to pay back all of her friends in whose weddings she had participated. Today they have two children and are expecting a third. They both want a big family, so they haven't decided if it will be their last.

Both couples, Marilyn and Jonathan and Celeste and Scott, represent successful transitions from *heart marriage* to committed marriage. Most people would have given up on these relationships long before the wedding date, but in both cases, the couple knew more than anyone else about their emotional commitments to each other. They were definitely heart married, having been monogamous and sexually intimate, they were together for four years in the case of Marilyn and Jonathan and ten years for Celeste and Scott. Interestingly, neither couple cohabited. Although they certainly spent many nights together over the span of their relationships, they kept their own residences. It certainly appears this could have been a factor allowing Marilyn and Celeste to act independently and, in effect, to turn the relationship around. In both relationships it is obvious, particularly for the men, that rather than coming closer to marriage, there was a growing reluctance with each passing year. This is a key sign of *heart marriage*. These two couples were stuck, unable to move forward, but unable to sever their relationships.

It is important to note, however, that in these two *heart marriages*, the signs of *heart divorce*, as we have defined them, were not pervasive. Except over the subject of marriage, these couples didn't experience persistent arguments and disagreements. They never really had doubts about their love for each other and therefore were not preoccupied with frequent thoughts of leaving. Their relationships were comfortable and except when Marilyn and Celeste longed for marriage, they did not experience the typical feelings of general uneasiness about the relationship. The final red flag indicating the need for a *heart divorce*, the inability to plan for the future, certainly was part of the dynamics of these two relationships. At close examination, however, these two couples had a pretty clear picture of what their futures would look like. They knew their feelings around children, commitment to marriage, whether they both would continue to work, where they would like to live, and many of the issues that couples discuss as part of their future planning. The real difficulty in these two relationships was, in fact, one person being unable to take the final step.

What should be noted is that these two examples are in stark contrast to the other examples shared throughout this book where *heart marriage* drove couples into doomed marriages. In these cases, *heart divorce* would have been the best choice, saving them from what they most feared—a failed marriage and divorce. In the examples of Marilyn and Jonathan and Celeste and Scott, all three conditions outlined earlier in the chapter that appear to support the transition from *heart marriage* to the long term legal commitment of marriage were present. First, in neither case did any of the four individuals doubt their love for each other, even the two who could not make the commitment to marriage. When friends and relatives questioned their love, they remained adamant that they loved their partner and knew that this was the person they wanted to marry when the time came. As with any couple, they may have seen things in each other that created difficulties and about which they had to make adjustments, but their love was never in question. Therefore, the typical doubts often ignored by heart married couples which signal an unhealthy relationship and an unlikely future were not present with these two heart married couples.

Secondly, with these two couples, each of the women courageously overcame her fear of making waves. Both boldly acknowledged their secret longing and desire to marry and expressed unhappiness with the relationships as they were. They basically made it clear what they wanted and that they were ready for the next step. This admission and subsequent honesty has to occur in order to begin the transition from *heart marriage* to the legal union of marriage. However, this successful transition doesn't happen simply because one person openly reveals the desire to marry. It is the third condition, whereby one person decides to act independently regardless of the consequences that completes the process and makes the transition possible.

The decision to take independent action typically takes shape in one or two ways. The person desiring the change either chooses to leave the relationship without issuing any ultimatums or elects to stay but does so determined to respectfully resist coaxing or cajoling the reluctant partner. Action of this nature signals taking responsibility for, and owning, one's choices without regard for the consequences to the relationship or the reaction of the other partner. Whereas ultimatums are typically issued in the hope that the partner will "wake up" and make a change; in this case, the person leaves in order to act in one's own best interest. He or she truly leaves the relationship to start a new life and most often that is exactly what happens. However, there are times when the partner who is stuck, given the space and time to gain insight, reaches the point that a proposal is possible. This is what happened with Jonathan when Marilyn finally took an honest stand and acted in her best interest even if it meant losing the person whom she knew she loved. Jonathan was able to think about and work through his own fears, and happily did so before it was too late for his relationship with Marilyn to be rekindled.

In the case of Celeste, the action she took was to stay in the relationship but with a new attitude of honesty and responsibility. When Celeste took responsibility for her decision to stay with Scott even though he would not make a move, she faced the fact that this was indeed her choice. No one was coercing or making her stay. In a real way, this acknowledgement gave her the freedom to decide to leave if that became necessary for her best interest. In the present, she trusted Scott's love for her and his eventual desire to marry and was able to proceed without resentment. This allowed her to respect Scott's position and to leave behind constantly hinting, coaxing, and nagging about all of her friends marrying. When she became melancholy about the subject, she dealt with it openly and made her decision regarding the relationship one day at a time. Of course, there was the risk that it would not turn out so happily. Scott may have never become ready for marriage and Celeste could have found herself down the road another several years decreasing her window of opportunity to safely have children. Fortunately, Celeste's new attitude of personal responsibility gave Scott the room he needed. He was able to look at his life and determine that he too was ready to embrace the future with Celeste that he had always known he eventually wanted. In both of these examples, the decision to act independently was the condition that made the difference and created the environment where these *heart marriages* transitioned into fulfilling legal marriages.

It goes without saying that relationships are complex and to assume that there are no exceptions when studying their dynamics is foolhardy. The examples given in this chapter certainly indicate that it is possible for *heart marriage* to result in a committed relationship intended to last a lifetime. In fact, it is likely that more *heart marriages* will make that transition if individuals consider the conditions presented in this chapter. Each is encouraged to recognize when they are heart married, assess whether or not *heart divorce* is warranted, and if not, make the decision to be open about their desire to marry, and take independent action. To help determine whether you are involved in a *heart marriage* that could become the committed marriage that you desire, take the quiz below.

TRANSITION QUIZ: CAN YOUR HEART MARRIAGE BECOME A COMMITTED MARRIAGE?

Directions: Answer yes or no to the following questions about your relationship.

1. Are you frustrated with your relationship, but still feel certain about the love you and your partner have for each other?

2. Have you been open with your boy/girlfriend about your desire to marry one day and your unwillingness to go on forever without a commitment; or has your partner had that honest discussion with you?

3. Would you say that your relationship is basically good—no major arguments or disagreements, except when you bring up getting married?

4. Do you feel like you know what your partner ultimately wants out of life and that it is compatible with your goals and desires?

5. Have you or your partner considered, threatened, or actually broken up for a fairly significant period of time because even though you love him/her, there is no movement toward a committed future?

6. In the midst of your frustration, has the thought crossed your mind that even though you want to be married, you would rather be with your boy/girlfriend unmarried than to be married to someone else?

7. Do you or your partner express the desire to marry one day, yet verbalize doubts, fears, or legitimate reasons for waiting?

8. Have you or your partner ever said to the other, "I love you and want to be with you, but do what you have to do because I'm just not ready to get married"?

9. Do friends and family tell you that you should break up with your boy/girlfriend, but you still believe that you will marry one day?

10. When you think about what you want in a relationship, does yours measure up in most every way except for the fact that you aren't married?

Scoring Key

❤ If you answered yes to five questions, there is hope for your relationship.

❤ If you answered yes to eight questions, it is very possible that your *heart marriage* can make the transition into a committed legal marriage.

❤ If you answered yes to Question ten only, it is worth taking some independent action that could result in your *heart marriage* making the transition to the committed marriage that you desire.

TAKING IT TO HEART: A CALL TO ACTION

❤ Talk seriously and openly with your girl/boyfriend about your desire to be married, and ask for an honest response about his/her plans. Encourage your partner not to simply tell you what he/she thinks you want to hear.

❤ Have the courage to take responsibility for your own unhappiness with the static position of the relationship and quit complaining, nagging, begging, or issuing ultimatums.

❤ Take action. Either stay and enjoy the relationship as it is until you are sure that is no longer a viable option for you, or leave the relationship and follow the suggestions outlined in chapter 8 under Step Four: Decide Upon an Intentional Plan to Move Forward.

12

Happily Ever After

You Have the Power to Make It Happen

I SN'T "HAPPILY EVER AFTER" what everyone dreams of and strives for? But is it only a fairy tale—one that is rare in the real world of marriages that seem to begin with so much promise yet too frequently end in divorce? Or does "happily ever after" apply to one's relationship and marriage at all? Maybe happiness once you are married is really more about what happens before marriage or regardless of marriage. In other words, perhaps "happily ever after" has to start with you!

The premise of this book is that *heart marriage* is a phenomenon that is increasing in today's environment with the loosening of attitudes around cohabitation and the increase of early sexual intimacy before marriage. We hypothesize that *heart marriage* can, and frequently does, result in the unhealthy decision to marry legally. We have discussed that when a couple acts married by being monogamous, sexually active, cohabiting, and maintaining a relationship over a prolonged period of time, the heart marries. Once the heart marries, any reluctance to actually walk down the aisle is a red flag, signaling that something is amiss in the relationship. Because the same strong bond that forms when a couple is married also forms in the case of *heart marriage,* many couples often feel compelled to tie the knot, even when a part of them is screaming, "No." Many times at least one member of the outwardly happy couple knows things "aren't right" but pushes the thought away long enough to travel the path to the altar.

There was a time, in the fairly recent past, when our mothers would warn us against premarital sex with the old saying, "Don't get the cart before the horse." Although a simple admonition and usually very pointed in its implication, there still is profound wisdom in those words from a broader standpoint. This book asserts that when couples allow the "heart to marry" before there has been an intentional and rational decision to accompany the emotional decision, then truly, the cart is trying to carry its load without the strength and power to propel and guide it. Awareness of the phenomenon of *heart marriage* makes it possible to act rationally and responsibly on your own behalf in these important issues of the heart and to save yourself wasted years and a great deal of heartache.

No doubt, because of the interplay between heart and head, it is difficult to make good relationship decisions. Young people today are bombarded in the media with the concept of love at first sight and the idea of falling passionately and hopelessly in love. In fact, even classical literature supports that notion—remember Romeo and Juliet? The lives of celebrities as well as such modern iconic television series as *Sex In the City* reinforce this image by constantly depicting professional, smart women having sex as a matter of course and falling hopelessly in love, only to find out that it isn't the real thing. As a result of such romanticizing, we have been forced out of necessity to coin the term "falling out of love" to describe what happens when things begin to go sour in our relationships. If you are looking for happily ever after, "falling" in or out of love doesn't really make much sense in regard to longevity, commitment, and true contentment. Instead, moving steadfastly toward a loving relationship, though not as fanciful, typically leads to a much healthier future and at the same time, can be exciting, passionate, and exhilarating.

Against this backdrop of "falling in love," *heart marriage* is an example of "falling into marriage." Throughout this book you have seen examples illustrating that just because a couple who exchanges vows has been together for years and possibly even lived together, doesn't necessarily mean they didn't "fall into marriage." In fact, often it is just the opposite. The heart married couple, without clear communication about what they are getting into, falls into the patterns of marriage. Eventually it seems that getting married is the only thing to do. Friends and family assume that the couple has been together so long that they must know what they are doing and that marriage is a good decision. We have seen, however, that this is not the case in many *heart marriages*. These couples may have mentioned their dreams and hopes for the future and verbalized support for one another when they were overwhelmed with that cloud of romance and excitement and still trying to impress each other; however, as time goes on in *heart marriage,* more is left unsaid than clearly spoken. When conversation moves to future plans that create conflict or behavior begins to irritate rather than to amuse, the heart overrides the head and the couple wishfully thinks that it will all work out. Unfortunately, it often doesn't. The decision to avoid discussing with your partner issues that are meaningful to you, such as your values, goals, and vision for your future is not a sound path. Good relationship decisions are a product of both the heart and the head. Though maybe not as romantic, the two working together is a much better recipe for success.

The question then remains, "Is it realistic to believe that one can have a 'happily ever after life' and, if so, what can a person do and when should one start to create this healthy relationship future?" There is no fail-safe approach when it comes to issues of the heart, but there are three things that can go a long way toward fulfilling personal goals in regard to love and marriage. First, before you become heavily involved in a relationship, make a life plan. Take a careful look at yourself, your values and goals, and create a clear vision for your future based on what you discover. Secondly, if at all possible, avoid falling into *heart marriage.* Make intentional decisions about your dating behavior that you are comfortable with and can stick to. And, perhaps most important, fully embrace your own personal power to take charge of your life!

MAKE A PLAN AND CREATE A VISION FOR YOUR LIFE

Life is a journey with many twists and turns and not being able to predict the future keeps it interesting; so rather than try to nail down every specific, create a "big picture" plan that can guide you in your decision-making, including decisions about relationships. Such a plan begins with a firm foundation based on your core values, purpose in life, and a vision for what accomplishing that purpose might look like in the coming years. Because relationships are such an important part of life, what you desire from your most intimate relationship is an important part of your vision for the future. Though we may try, our life goals and relationships, love, and marriage simply cannot be separated. Instead, they must complement each other. Good decisions about relationships take into account the other aspects of an individual's vision for the future. To make a life plan that does not include purposeful consideration about whether you see yourself married and, if so, what you want from that relationship along with the important "givens" your life partner must possess is dangerous.

To create your unique and personal vision for the future, you may ask yourself a variety of questions. What do you value most in life? Do you have an overarching goal? Do you want to get married or have a career or both? Are you going to college and do you want to earn an advanced degree? Is it important to you that you complete your education before you enter into marriage? Do you wish to have children and would you consider adopting if you find that you can't have a child naturally? Do you value your faith and want to be a part of a church or spiritual community? Are you most interested in being involved in work or a profession that serves the greater good of the community regardless of the financial prospect, or are you most interested in building financial wealth and enjoying the finer material things in life? If you are a female, do you want to work after you have children? If you are a male, would you mind your wife earning more money than you and would you consider staying home with children? Do you value fidelity and faithfulness in a marriage? Are you looking for a partner who is intellectually stimulating? Is it important to you to have interests that you and your partner share so that you spend your recreational and leisure time together? Do you have standards of behavior that you believe apply to married couples? Do you believe that honesty and truth are always the best choice, or do you feel that sometimes it's better that one doesn't know what might hurt them? Are you a saver or a spender? Do you believe it is important in a marriage for both partners to work and maintain their own interests? Is your vision of marriage one of equality with both parties making decisions together, or do you have a vision of marriage where the husband is the main breadwinner and primary decision-maker?

As you answer these questions, you begin to paint a vivid picture of your future—a roadmap to follow that will guide you in creating a meaningful and fulfilling life. If being married is a part of that picture, it is critical that you discuss these values, dreams, and issues openly and unashamedly with any potential partner. Verbalizing your expectations and inviting your partner to do likewise will elicit information that can either encourage you to pursue the relationship further or send up red flags. The caveat is that for the greatest chance of success, this sharing process should come before you begin to practice the behaviors that bind your hearts emotionally and create *heart marriage*. Clearly articulating who you are, what you value, and what you want out of life, as well as discerning whether the person you are dating fits that vision before the relationship becomes prolonged and before you have become deeply bound through sexual intimacy or living together, will enable you to make wiser and more reasoned decisions about your relationships. It will also prevent *heart marriage* and the heartache that ensues.

Unfortunately, counter to all wisdom, women and men alike often have a vision or plan for their life that includes marriage, but ignore it when they become attracted to someone and begin to date. They date a guy or a girl whom they readily admit doesn't complement their vision or fit the profile of who they believe would be a good marriage partner. They may tell themselves that it doesn't matter because they aren't ready to make a commitment, but before they know it they are involved in the behaviors that bind the heart together, which is like playing with fire. If you want to be married, the wisest decision is to date the kind of person that you can see yourself marrying. Keeping your vision front and center in your mind, listening to all the signals, and being true to your plan within the context of relationships allows you to be in charge of your life in a positive and forceful way and brings you closer to a "happily ever after" future.

Understand that including key aspects of relationships in your life plan is not intended to remove the suspense and mystery from love and attraction. Relationship decisions are neither simply rational nor totally emotional. Attraction, physical connection, and passion are important to a relationship; but those things fade if the partner doesn't share your values, have compatible dreams, and support your life's purpose. Conversely, sharing those things over time and committing to continue to know, understand, and support one another will not only keep the flames of love and passion burning; it will fan the fire, enabling it to burn brighter.

Now, let's take a look at two young women who illustrate the importance of having a vision and allowing it to guide relationship decisions. Their stories also illustrate that it is important to do this before *heart marriage* occurs. The encouraging news is that the intentional act of creating a vision and a plan for your life can actually help prevent *heart marriage*. Both of these examples end with promise, but one was much more painful getting there.

BEVERLY ANN

Beverly Ann lit up a room when she entered. Her silky honey blond hair framed her face like a halo. She was gentle, kind, and sincere with everyone she met, and if that wasn't enough, she also was a *summa cum laude* graduate from an Ivy League school. After graduation, she worked for a year in D.C. for a nonprofit "think tank" and decided that she would pursue a graduate degree in public policy and international relations. She knew this would likely take her out of the country for awhile but the thought was exciting. Even though she had a wonderful family and was close to her parents and two siblings, she wanted to experience new places and new people. Just as everyone had anticipated from the time Beverly Ann was a young child, she had everything anyone would want. That is, everything except a boyfriend. She was about to turn thirty and her friends and family didn't understand why she wasn't engaged or married. In fact everyone else appeared to be much more worried about this than Beverly Ann. When asked, she would acknowledge that she wanted to be married one day and hopefully have children, but would rather be alone than in a bad relationship or sacrifice her plans for the future.

Although she was a bit of a late bloomer on the dating scene and didn't have boyfriends in high school, she had plenty of dates in college and as many as she wanted as a young professional woman. She found it difficult to meet her equal intellectually and when she did, he often did not possess the traditional values that she held dear, such as family, faith, integrity, and fidelity in relationships and marriage. In D.C., it was easy to find ambitious men, but many were more driven by the desire for wealth and personal acclaim than Beverly Ann. She was simply an unusual combination of one who was extremely bright and competent, motivated by a desire to accomplish important but good work in society, and yet grounded with the traditional values of her southern family and upbringing. Occasionally, Beverly Ann would date a fellow for several months and her parents became hopeful, but the relationship would end for one reason or the other. Sometimes it was because she realized that they weren't on the same page on important issues and sometimes it ended because the guy would determine that Beverly Ann was a prude and uninterested in having a good time. Beverly Ann did not sleep around and wouldn't consider cohabiting. She knew what she wanted in life and in a mate; and also intuitively knew that for her it would be foolish to become intimate with someone she would not want to marry. Although most all of her friends were married and having children, Beverly Ann was content and very hopeful that one day she would meet a man with whom she could share her life.

Beverly Ann is an example of a woman with a plan and a vision for her life that includes marriage, but not at the expense of her values and goals. She might appear inflexible and too selective to those around her, but she is comfortable with her level of discernment. She knows herself and what she wants and believes that in time, she would find it. The difference in Beverly Ann and many other women is that early in her life she clearly articulated for herself her vision for the future. Because she dated sparingly until college she had time to observe others and make some wise decisions about her dating behavior. She didn't believe in sex before marriage or cohabiting, but was practical about it at her age and had never strictly said that under no circumstances would it ever happen. What she did understand was that because these behaviors meant something special to her, it would be dangerous to practice them unless the person she was with was a real potential marriage partner. Beverly Ann's vision for her future and her decisions around dating behavior had so far shielded her both from *heart marriage* and from making bad relationship choices. Some might say they also had kept her still single in her early thirties, but Beverly Ann remained optimistic. Her "happily ever after" life was in the present tense and although it might later be enriched by marriage, she was at peace with herself.

ELLEN AND ANDREW

Friends made Ellen's world go around even as a young girl. Her young face carried the hint of the woman she would become—full of life, fun, and emotion. Often the center of attention, Ellen grew to depend upon her ability to be liked and make people happy. Her exterior was bubbly, positive, and confident. She was smart and outspoken, but that sometimes got her into trouble with her friends and made her appear overbearing. She performed well in school, but decided that smart would not be her most visible trait. She was a helper, a rescuer, a mediator. Ellen liked to find the broken and put them back together. She had secret doubts about herself and being important to someone else helped her overcome that. She felt the most useful with the underdog and was a champion for anyone who had potential. It was that way with her relationships too.

In high school, Ellen had lots of boys who were her buddies, but only one boyfriend throughout high school. The relationship was a mystery to her friends and family. Andrew was as quiet as she was talkative. She was in the most popular crowd and heavily involved in school activities, and he was accepted, but on the fringes. It was a given that she would go to college. He was not unintelligent, but had little interest in college and wanted to go straight to work, even though he didn't know what that would be. She thrived in her church youth group and was a leader in a Christian outreach organization. He was a believer, but had little interest in those activities. Andrew had some family problems and Ellen prided herself in her empathy and acceptance. The main attraction for Ellen was that this young man seemed to love and look up to her. They were not sexually intimate, but were monogamous and the relationship lasted two and a half years. They finally broke up just before college, but the ill fit between the life path that Ellen would most naturally want and what this young man had to offer was a precursor of what was to come.

It was her last year in college and Ellen was still a good student and a business major, but really didn't have a burning desire for a career. She enjoyed working, was good at anything she did, and always impressed her boss in summer internships. She knew what she wanted most was to marry and have children, but rarely mentioned it because most of her friends were preparing to aggressively pursue careers or graduate school. She wasn't overly materialistic, but was accustomed to having pretty much anything she wanted and was very generous with others. In her mind, love was absolutely the most important thing in a relationship and the rest would take care of itself.

When Ellen met Andrew the sparks flew. He was cute, smart, and artistically talented. Having lots of potential, but no direction, Andrew dropped out of college and was working construction to pay his bills. He made pretty good money when he worked, but the work wasn't steady. When they met, he mentioned plans to go back to school, but had some fear about getting started. Ellen had another project—Andrew just needed a little boost and seemed to appreciate Ellen's encouragement. They were having sex within a month of their first date and began to spend a lot of time together. They were in love. He began to spend most nights with

Ellen at her apartment. Basically, they were living together, but he technically had another space. As soon as she graduated and rented a house, he expected to move in with her on her dime. She resisted his moving in completely, though they continued to spend most nights together. He resented her decision and accused her of being selfish. A year later, he still had not returned to school. He was becoming more and more clingy and had become negative about the things that Ellen cared about. She even began to sense that he didn't believe in God, but was afraid to ask because she wasn't sure she wanted to know. The guy who had adored her now put her down and tried to shake her confidence. They began to fight and broke up several times. Even though her friends were thrilled, she always went back to him. Even knowing that he could not give her what she wanted in life, she just couldn't seem to break it off. Ellen continued to think that she could fix the problem. When, after three years, Andrew quit his job and made little effort to find another one, Ellen broke up with him for the final time.

She wanted to make it stick and knew she needed help, so got into counseling and began to discover the unhealthy role she played as a rescuer. The therapist asked her to project out to the next ten years and write a detailed summary of the future she wanted. Ellen conscientiously put into words what she knew but hadn't clearly articulated. She saw herself as a happily married woman and a stay-at-home mom who was involved with the church and her children's school. She wanted to be able to provide her children with what they needed, take family vacations, and live in a comfortable home. She was willing to work and help, and perhaps run a small business from home, but she didn't want to be the primary breadwinner. Friends and family were important to her, and she knew that she needed a partner who also valued these relationships and wanted to share them with her.

Realizing that her need to rescue continued to put her with men who did not fit this profile and who could not enhance her life's goal, she decided that she needed to work on herself and make a change. Not only did she decide that she had to make better choices as to who she dated, she had to change *how* she dated. Her inability to break off this unhealthy relationship was because she had become heart married. Her almost immediate sexual involvement with Andrew and their practically cohabiting had contributed to that. Even though she didn't discuss it with Andrew, she realized that in a way she was "playing married," hoping it could become the real thing. She was grateful that Andrew was in no position to ask her to marry him, because she feared that she would have said yes. Ellen vowed that she would not get emotionally entangled again with someone so wrong for her, and that meant taking the time to explore the important issues she identified through creating her vision. It also meant delaying a sexual relationship and avoiding living together. She wanted to remain independent and to take care of herself, but not carry the load for someone else. Andrew continued to pursue her for several months, but she held firm. The relationship ended for good after three and a half years.

Ellen and Andrew were heart married, and it was very painful to break up. Though Ellen was suffering, with the help of family, friends, and her therapist, she was able to make the decision to sever the relationship. Ellen had some personal issues to resolve, but in regard to her relationship, not only had she practiced the behaviors of marriage—monogamy, sexual intimacy, and basically cohabiting—she did so without considering her vision for the future. She had a vision that was loosely conceived, but had never clearly articulated it to herself and certainly not to Andrew. If she dared to do so, Andrew came up short as a partner, so she pushed it out of her mind. Unlike Beverly Ann who carefully established her course in life before becoming involved in a love interest that enabled her to avoid unhealthy relationships, Ellen's path to establishing and following a clear vision for her future was a rocky one. She experienced *heart marriage* and heartache, but once she began to allow her life plan to dictate relationship decisions, she too was hopeful and optimistic. Thankfully, this *heart marriage* did not end in a legal union and Ellen created for herself a second chance, armed with a clearer vision for a fulfilling future.

DECIDE YOUR DATING BEHAVIOR BEFOREHAND —NOT AS YOU GO

Even with a clear vision for a wonderful and fulfilling future, if you allow yourself to become intimately bound to a partner before knowing each other well and without honestly exploring the important issues that will affect your future, you put yourself at risk of *heart marriage*. Reason goes out the window; wishful thinking sets in; obligation and inevitability becomes the engine that drives you to the altar; and the pathway to your goals becomes very rocky and ultimately leads to a dead end. Since *heart marriage* threatens your future happiness, in order to insure a "happily ever after" life you must not only create your vision, but also make dating behavior decisions that will help you both avoid *heart marriage* and reach your goals.

Chapter 9 discussed ways to avoid *heart marriage* and indicated that the safest way is to delay sexual intimacy and cohabitation until marriage. Delaying sexual intimacy for a period of time allows a couple to get to know one another intellectually and socially, letting the relationship grow and mature before binding the couple through sex. The very nature of the sexual desire and sexual intimacy requires that an individual make this important decision before the relationship begins. Most important, it demands that one have the courage and resolve to stick to it. In order to make such decisions, an individual must first buy into the belief that early engagement in a sexual relationship binds the heart prematurely and can be detrimental to sound decision-making. This decision also dictates that one recognizes the value of reserving the sexual relationship for marriage or at least until a relationship is serious and likely to move toward marriage. In an effort to help you avoid *heart marriage*, chapter 9 also discusses the wisdom of choosing not to cohabit prior to marriage. Similarly, if one makes the decision not to cohabit, it is important to make it early, before dating seriously and practicing monogamy.

Recalling Jennifer and Lance, Sherith and Ben, and Cristina and Tommy

Remember the couples introduced in chapter 9? At least one member of each of these twosomes made the decision to refrain from sexual intimacy before marriage as well as cohabitation, although there were variations in how they handled the implementation of those decisions.

Both Jennifer and Sherith believed that sex should be reserved for marriage and were committed to waiting. They made these decisions early, most likely even before they started dating, and both got through high school and college without becoming sexually intimate. Jennifer, though physically quite beautiful herself, was disillusioned with the emphasis on external beauty and sexuality, and even considered a life of celibacy. She completed college, began a career, and was very involved in her community church when she met Lance. She was, however, determined to be true to her decision and as an adult woman she adopted a model for dating called courting that would insure that her decision to abstain from sex and cohabitation would be upheld. Even her family was skeptical, but she held firm to her decision and Lance agreed. The fact that Lance respected her values and decision and was willing to date her on those terms was a real indication of his desire to know and understand her as she was. In this case it worked and the two were married. Had he not been willing, however, Jennifer knew what she wanted; she had made her decision and was prepared to live by it.

Sherith, though just as strong in her decision to remain a virgin until marriage and refrain from cohabitation, had a more traditional courtship with Ben. She had suffered a broken heart in college, but she wasn't heart married. Although the college heartache was painful and caused her to question her judgment, her original vision of reserving sexual intimacy for her husband remained in tact. Through the experience, Sherith had learned that she needed to be totally honest, not just in discussing her life's goals and her personal and professional commitment to service and social justice, but also about her values, hopes, and fears around relationships. Her open and honest communication with Ben and the decisions she had made around sexual intimacy and cohabitation together played an important part in the purposeful way their relationship developed. Holding fast to her values and being confident in her decisions, she was straightforward in presenting these to Ben and found that he shared the same ideas and values. They acknowledged their sexual desires but because they were equally committed to their decision to reserve sexually intimacy for their marriage partner, they were able to be physical with each other while respecting the boundaries they had established. They chose to have intercourse a short time before their wedding day, but their communication remained open, clear, and honest; and each step taken toward their marriage was very intentional.

Cristina was a different story. Her decision to refrain from sex and cohabitation came later, after a number of relationships, some serious and others not so serious, which involved sex. She came to the conclusion that early and casual sexual intimacy changes a relationship and often not for the better. She decided she didn't want to do that again and made a clear decision in her mind about sex and future relationships. Her decision, unlike Jennifer and Sherith, however, was not necessarily to wait until marriage. She wanted to delay sexual intimacy the next time around until the relationship had developed and she felt that it was going somewhere. She wanted to know that she cared deeply about her partner first without the emphasis being on sex. Because this was a new decision and behavior is habitual, she wasn't sure she could stick with it when she met Tommy. Although she didn't announce the decision on the first date, she was honest with Tommy when the time came and he was willing to respect her wishes to delay a sexual relationship. Later, when the opportunity to live together arose, she again asserted her decision to remain in her own space, fearing that this could be the final straw. It wasn't. Their relationship had developed to the point that it was worth it to Tommy to comply with her decision. More than that, he went on to ask her to marry him. His willingness to support and respect her wishes spoke volumes to her as to the kind of husband he would be.

The decisions these couples made may not be the norm in our society today, but they are reemerging and becoming more prevalent. Without question, it is difficult to make such choices, especially the longer the couple delays marriage. Clearly articulating and communicating decisions about sex and cohabiting and reaching an agreement as the relationship begins to develop makes it much more likely that one will abide by them. There is often the fear, particularly among women, that a potential partner will be turned off or the person you love will end the relationship. It is a risk that many don't want to take. In order to make this choice successfully, it is critical that you strongly believe it is important for your partner to respect your decisions, that you expect this respect from anyone you date seriously or consider a potential marriage partner, and that you will settle for nothing less. Although there is no guarantee that all will turn out as you would like, having the firm belief that without this level of respect a relationship is not worthy of your commitment will help quell your fear and give you comfort and peace in the midst of disappointment if your fears become a reality.

EMBRACE YOUR PERSONAL POWER
TO MAKE YOUR LIFE WHAT YOU WANT IT TO BE

ANNETTE AND JOSEPH

She did it! It was the hardest thing she had ever done, but she did it. She broke up and this time for good. When she talked about it, she expressed a little nervousness with her hands and her eyes revealed a tinge of sadness, but she spoke with more clarity and confidence than she had in years about her future and what she wanted from it. Yes, she was approaching thirty and alone after a six-year relationship, but Annette was at peace and free of the nagging doubt that had plagued her for at least the last three of those six. It had been four months since the final breakup (there had been several before) and she was holding fast to her conviction, resisting all temptation to call or have that "innocent" meeting just to talk that always turned into tears and resulted in "making up." She was beginning to feel optimistic about her future and was looking forward, with a bit of fear and trepidation, to pursuing new relationships. She had met a few guys and been on a few dates, but none had panned out as yet. Her friends accused her of being too picky, but this time, she knew what she wanted—and just as important, what she didn't want.

Annette was a "head turner" with curly chestnut hair and a petite, curvy figure. She carried herself with dignity and projected confidence. Determined to be successful, she was moving up the corporate ladder as a businesswoman, always sought ways to strengthen her management and leadership skills, and even found time to do volunteer work. Her mother had multiple sclerosis from the time she was a young girl and as the oldest of three children, Annette had grown up very independent, fending for herself, and often taking care of the household. When she lost her mother in her third year of college, she turned to Joseph for support and he was more than willing to give it to her. He was kind and devoted and filled an important gap. Neither of them were virgins, but they were not promiscuous. Annette had only one sexual encounter early in college with a guy she had a huge crush on and Joseph had a couple of casual lovers. Between the two of them, however, sexual intimacy seemed to come naturally and they were intimate within a few months of dating. The affection was comforting and Annette thought she had found the person she wanted to marry.

When college was over, they both moved back home, which turned out to be the same city, though they hadn't known each other before college. Joseph got a job in sports public relations and Annette landed a job with an up and coming firm in the fast paced world of wealth management. Annette and Joseph talked about marriage, but wanted to get established in their careers first and Annette knew that she didn't want to live together unless they were married. They rented separate apartments, even though Joseph thought it was rather foolish, but they spent many nights together.

Over time, it became obvious that Annette was much more driven toward success than Joseph. She bought her first home, a lovely spacious English Tudor in the suburbs with three bedrooms, a two-car garage, and a large back yard. Joseph didn't like some of the demands placed on him at work and suddenly decided to quit his job and freelance, but it was soon evident that he didn't have the drive to push himself. He was content with what he had while Annette wanted to advance in her career and become a contributor in the life of the community. He was good to Annette and would do anything she asked of him, but that was just it—he always waited for her to take the initiative and tell him what to do. At times she felt like Joseph's sister and not his lover.

Rather than talk about marriage like she had in the past, a growing reluctance surfaced. There were several other things that began to bother her. Since she made more money and could afford more, he seemed content to let her pay and even quit offering to pitch in. He seemed to resent the time she spent at work and didn't appear to connect that with her earnings. He was proud of her accomplishments, but complained when her extra efforts with community initiatives interfered with their time together. Annette felt like Joseph was a part of her and she cared for him, yet found herself instigating arguments to give herself an excuse to break up. This happened several times, but they would both cry and feel terribly lonely; Joseph would show up on her doorstep; and she would give in. She even would say out loud to herself, "Why not marry him. He is good to me. I'm not getting any younger and he is faithful." It wouldn't take long, though, and the same nagging feelings of doubt and foreboding crept back in. She would have to be the motivator in the family, and she did not want that role. She wanted more. Annette pulled herself together and had an open and honest talk with Joseph. She asked him to take all of his belongings from her house. After six years, their relationship was over. At the beginning of this story, you find her four months later, still a little shaky, but growing stronger everyday. Annette was at peace, knowing she had done the right thing.

Annette did what is very difficult to do. She took charge of her life and broke off a long-term relationship that already felt like a marriage. Why was this so hard when she knew that it wasn't the kind of relationship she wanted? Like the many other couples you have met in this book, without realizing it, she had become heart married and felt paralyzed. She knew that she would like to have children and that the clock was ticking, but she also knew that the person she married needed to be on the same track. She had ambition and believed in striving for excellence. She valued hard work, success, and continuous learning. Although she grew up in a comfortable situation, she felt each generation should do better than the last. Love was important to her, of course, but she didn't want to struggle financially or constantly feel the need to push her husband. Her career was moving at a fast pace and she enjoyed the challenge and the responsibility. She wanted to have an impact in her community as well as a partner with whom she could share that zeal. When she began to realize it wasn't Joseph, she felt stuck. She certainly loved him in a comfortable way. They had become friends. He had been there for her when she needed him. But she also knew that Joseph was satisfied with just getting by and didn't mind depending on her. She could see trouble ahead. Their different paths were taking them further apart and diminishing the love they felt for each other.

She had a decision to make. It would be so easy to get married, since Joseph was willing. She could try to make it work, have children, and end up feeling the same feelings ten years down the road; or, she could take charge and do what she knew needed to be done. This wasn't easy. She wondered if she could start all over. How long would it take to meet some-one else? By the time she met someone and the relationship developed, would it be too late to have children? Would she break up and find that she really loved Joseph after all? Annette had to be able to live with these unanswered questions before she broke off her relationship. Because it was actually a *heart divorce,* she had to actively and purposefully fill her time to help with the loneliness. She couldn't be sure that she would achieve that "happily ever after" future that everyone wants, but decided to get off the roller coaster of trying to make an unhealthy relationship work. She took charge of her life and began to proceed carefully and intention-ally. For Annette taking charge meant getting a *heart divorce.* Annette was stuck in a *heart marriage,* but gave herself another chance—a chance to realize her goals, her hopes, and dreams.

ACT NOW TO FIND A FUTURE YOU DESERVE

This book makes the fairly safe assumption that a loving and enduring relationship that enriches our lives is universally sought after. In order to grow and mature, this kind of relationship requires spending considerable time together. Romance and attraction are also important elements of such love and caring, and respectful sexual intimacy strengthens and enhances the relationship. The ability to commit to one person and approach the commitment with fidelity is also a key part of such a relationship. The very notion of a committed relationship implies monogamy. With all of this in mind, you may be asking if there is really any problem with the phenomenon we call *heart marriage,* which occurs when all of these elements come together? Remember, the key factor that sets *heart marriage* apart from a healthy relationship is that these heart binding behaviors occur either before or in the absence of clearly articulated and intentional decision-making that joins the passion of the heart and sensibility of the mind.

Although love must be the centerpiece, a healthy and enduring relationship is not based solely on love. A healthy relationship is about knowing who you are, what you value, and what you want for your life; and then matching that with an individual who supports and enhances your vision. It goes without saying that this person should be someone you enjoy and to whom you are attracted. Amazingly, when you share core values and support each other's goals, attraction grows and love develops and deepens. *Heart marriage,* on the other hand, just happens over time. Emotions typically lead to behavior that binds a couple and they feel married without the important rational considerations that make a relationship sound and equipped for the long haul. When a couple doesn't share the same values or support each other's dreams and goals, the opposite of what happens in a healthy relationship occurs. The flames of love dim and attraction becomes a distant memory, yet a couple is still emotionally bound and stuck trying to make a bad situation right.

The extraordinary news is that you have within you the power to forge an intentional path to a fulfilling future that includes love and an intimate relationship. You just have to make the intentional decision to do it. Falling in love in the short term is exciting, but falling into *heart marriage* is a bruising tumble that you don't want nor have to take. You can choose to walk steadfastly into your most intimate relationship and enjoy each detail along the way. If you will spend the time to know yourself and what you are looking for in a committed relationship, make decisions around dating that prevent the unintentional marrying of the heart, and exercise your personal power to take charge of your life, there is no end to the happiness that is in store for you. Regardless of where you are with your relationships—whether you are just beginning your adventure into dating or have already fallen prey to a *heart marriage* that requires firm intervention—the time to start doing these things is now. It's never too late!

Taking It to Heart: A Call to Action

❤ Make a list of the things you value in life and then go back and circle no more than five that are the most important. These are your core values. Ask yourself if you are honoring those values with your behavior?

❤ Find a quiet place and think about where you want to be five and then ten years from now. Create a word picture of your future. What is your most hopeful vision? Step out there and be as specific as possible in the various areas of your life. Be sure to cover your work and career life, your family life, your spiritual life, leisure and recreation, and anything else of importance to you.

❤ When thinking about a life partner, consider the kind of person who could help you realize the vision you created. What traits would he or she need to possess? What would get in your way or be a stumbling block to your happiness and the fulfillment of your dreams?

❤ If you are in a relationship, do an honest assessment in view of your most hopeful vision. If it is complementary, you are on the right track. If it isn't, you know what to do.

❤ Go for it!

Frequently Asked Questions

ARE FAMOUS UNMARRIED COUPLES like Oprah and Stedman or Goldie Hawn and Kurt Russell heart married? If so, how have their relationships lasted so long and are you saying their relationships are unhappy?

No outsider looking in can say whether or not a couple is heart married. The phenomenon of *heart marriage* is one that needs to be determined by the couple in question. In the case of famous couples, only their friends and family truly know the details of the relationship. Remember, too, that couples can be deeply bound together; even heart married, and not feel the need to get legally married. These couples may be happy and content with the relationship as it stands. Couples may be heart married and not have any of the signs that they need a *heart divorce*. More often, one of the individuals in the *heart marriage* will eventually desire to be legally married and the couple will have to navigate that shift in the relationship.

IT SEEMS LIKE ALMOST everyone in this day and age has premarital sex and lives together before marriage. It also seems that most of these couples eventually are happily married. Doesn't that go against the unhappiness described in *heart marriage*?

The four signs of *heart marriage* are sexual intimacy, cohabitation, monogamy, and reluctance to marry over time. All the signs do not have to be present for *heart marriage* to occur. Research shows a difference in the success of marriages preceded by cohabitation when the cohabitation is prenuptial. Prenuptial cohabitation is living together when there is an announced engagement and the wedding date is set. In *heart marriage*, there is no definite date for a wedding and the relationship just lingers on and on with a lot of uncertainty as to where the relationship is going. So while an engaged couple who is living together is intimately bound, by our definition they would not be heart married because the relationship is moving toward legal marriage in a defined and public way.

Has the concept of *heart marriage* been scientifically researched? The concept of *heart marriage* has not been scientifically researched. These are our observations as mothers, as a professional therapist, and as a registered nurse. When we shared this concept with friends, family, clients, and then strangers, we found the idea resonated very strongly with them and most could immediately recall someone they would describe as having been heart married. We hope that introducing this new concept into the lexicon and culture will result in research that will help couples navigate the emotions of the heart.

Who is most vulnerable to *heart marriage*? Certainly any couple who becomes sexually intimate, cohabits, and is monogamous without a commitment to the future is vulnerable, whether they are twenty or forty years old. However, as we have looked at *heart marriage* several things have been very interesting to learn. Statistics indicate that in the South, which is considered the Bible belt, people marry at an earlier age and divorce at a higher rate. We would hypothesize that young people who are brought up in a more religious atmosphere seek to get married after being sexually involved and cohabiting in an effort to bring their behavior into congruence with their values and religious teachings. The assumption might also be made that in the Bible belt states, more couples legally marry once they are heart married and then they quickly divorce. As the concept of *heart marriage* is understood, in the future, couples who are sexually intimate, monogamous, and heart married can dissolve their relationship through *heart divorce* rather than lengthen the breakup time and incur the added expense of legal marriage and then divorce.

Why does it matter if an individual heart marries many times to different people? There are a number of reasons that multiple *heart marriages* are unhealthy. The break up of *heart marriages* can be every bit as traumatic as legal divorce. These devastating breakups result in depression, the loss of self-esteem, and generalized problems in establishing good relationships. It is also known that the chances for a happy marriage are reduced as the number of marriages and divorces increase for an individual. In essence, the damage and hurt from multiple *heart divorces* is as destructive as that of multiple legal divorces. As a practical matter, since *heart marriages* are by definition prolonged relationships, multiple *heart marriages* are a waste of valuable time for a mature female who wishes to have a family and finds that she has squandered a considerable chunk of her child bearing years. While biologically men are able to procreate for more years than women, men can also experience the sense of lost time and opportunity if they hope to have a family before arriving at middle age or older. It is our hope by writing this book that people will protect themselves from this damaging behavior and put practices into place that will result in happy, healthy long term legal marriages.

DO MEN EXPERIENCE THE same pain as women when a *heart marriage* is dissolving and do the same strategies for negotiating a *heart divorce* and recovering from an unhealthy *heart marriage* apply to both men and women?

Men experience the confusion of *heart marriage* and the pain of *heart divorce* in the same ways that women do although they may cope differently. For example, women tend to verbalize their feelings to other women or family members, while men more often throw themselves into a new routine or activity to recover from the hurt of *heart divorce*. Although we have no absolute data to prove our observations, anecdotally we have noticed that women seem to be more likely to purchase and read books about relationships to gain insight and learn how to cope with their situations. They may encourage male partners to read the books that are helpful to them, but men often reject this type of resource until they sense that their relationship is truly in a crisis or near dissolution. Likewise, women tend to be more inclined to seek counseling to address relationship problems, while again men often agree to counseling only as a last resort when they sense that the relationship is literally "falling to pieces." We believe, however, that the suggestions found in this book for coping with the pain and frustration of *heart marriage*, negotiating *heart divorce*, and avoiding the *heart marriage* trap are equally as applicable and beneficial to men as they are to women.

WHAT IS THE DIFFERENCE in being heart married and just being "in love?" Aren't all couples who are in love heart married and doesn't it hurt just as much if you break up?

Love is not the differentiating factor in whether or not a couple is heart married. Neither is feeling pain when a couple breaks up. Most, if not all, heart married couples are "in love" but many couples who are "in love" are not heart married. The pivotal sign of *heart marriage*, after sexual intimacy, cohabitation, and monogamy, is that the relationship has gone on for a prolonged period of time, often years, yet the couple hasn't clearly and mutually discussed the desire to be married or made that commitment. In fact, often they have grown to avoid the question, even though one of the individuals in the relationship may want to marry. As time goes on, a real reluctance to marry develops. Nagging doubts and red flags plague the couple, but because the couple is silently but profoundly bound together in *heart marriage*, they tend to brush off, trivialize, or ignore those danger signals. It is true that breaking up is painful for any couple who has experienced sincere love for one another, whether heart married or not. However, when a heart married couple breaks up, the couple unfortunately misinterprets the intense pain and lets it convince them that breaking up was a mistake. True to their pattern of not communicating clearly and honestly, they often tragically give in and marry or else they may waste more years in a nonproductive and unhealthy relationship.

The couple that is "in love" and in a healthy relationship is indeed emotionally bound together in many ways. However, unlike heart married couples, they maintain open and clear communication; they recognize and process warning signs, moving to make sound decisions when they occur; and they are able to make plans for their future, both individually and together. If they break up, it can be very painful, but they recognize that it is normal to experience hurt for a period of time. Because they have a better sense that their decision was based on sound judgment, they are more confident to go through the healing process without jumping back into the relationship.

W HAT IS THE BEST way to avoid *heart marriage*?
 In the purest form, we would suggest that relationships start off slowly and develop over time into a deep friendship first. We also believe that individuals should examine their goals and values so that they are clear about what they want in life and relationships. This should be openly discussed with any serious dating partner throughout the relationship to insure that one's partner is preferably "on the same page" about the future or at the very least, aware of where each other stands. While it seems idealistic, and maybe unrealistic, in this post-sexual revolutionary world, we suggest that sexual intimacy be reserved for marriage or at least postponed until a couple is engaged to be married. We believe that early

sexual involvement adds an emotional dimension that can preclude objectivity and sound decision-making in a relationship. We have also concluded, generally speaking, that we do not recommend living together in a sexual relationship until married or engaged with a set date. The boundary of separate residences and bedrooms can keep the relationship more intentional and prevent falling into *heart marriage*. These things will help couples avoid the uncertainty of *heart marriage*.

A Note from the Authors

To OUR READERS, WE would like to say a final word on a personal level. First of all, we hope that something on these pages has resulted in one of those "aha" moments for you. Relationships are hard and no matter how sophisticated we become, there is nothing like the wonderful feeling of loving someone, trusting that person with your dreams, and walking together through life in pursuit of those dreams. If you picked this book up, we believe that you are seeking that kind of relationship.

As we worked on the book, occasionally we mustered our courage and shared the concepts with someone. To our delight, we began to find more and more folks, most often young women, who would "get it." An incredible moment occurred when one of us attended a leadership retreat and a young woman overheard a conversation about the book. She interrupted and emotionally blurted out, *"Oh my gosh, that's me. Tell me how I can negotiate a heart divorce with respect and kindness. I don't know how, but I know I have to do it."* It was at that point we knew that if even one person was able to forge a better relationship future from reading our book, it was worth the effort.

Don't get us wrong—there was some angst along the way, but we had fun. We're friends—we enjoy each other—and our teamwork was amazing. The longer we worked, our ideas became clearer. We became more convinced that this phenomenon we call *heart marriage* is real and does result in pain, anguish, and lost opportunities that can be prevented. When we began, we purposefully attempted to be neutral about the *heart marriage* signs. We didn't want to be judgmental and turn the readers off, before they got started. The longer we worked on the project, however, the stronger our belief grew that sexual intimacy and cohabitation before marriage is unwise and can cloud the real beauty of a committed marriage where both people have the best interest of the other on the "front burner." Although we intentionally chose not to write this as a Christian book, we became more convinced that God has a perfect plan for marriage—a plan where both individuals are honored and loved unselfishly. Most important, we believe that any individual who desires a full and committed relationship through marriage, regardless of their religious convictions, can benefit by understanding *heart marriage*.

We want to reiterate that we do not present this book as a scientific research study. No questionnaires were sent out, nor did we interview large numbers of individuals. Rather, this book is the result of a lifetime of observations and experiences that we have had in our professions, our friendships, our civic and volunteer activities, and our families. We do want to assure you that the stories you read throughout these pages and the people in them are real. They happened basically the way they are presented, although the names and some identifying details were changed to protect the privacy of the individuals.

Most important, we believe that you may find yourself in one of these stories and by all means, when you do, seize the moment—take charge of yourself—make the changes that will give you a fabulous future.

Lora and Barbara

Bibliography

Alternatives to Marriage Project, 2009. Online: http://www.unmarried.org/statistics
.html#numbers.

Aviv, Rachel. "On a Date With ...." *New York Times*, July 29, 2007, sec. Education Life, 31.

Centers for Disease Control and Prevention. "Sexually Transmitted Diseases Surveillance,"
2007. Online: http://www.cdc.gov/std/stats07/trends.htm.

———. "National Survey of Family Growth," 2002. Online: http://www.cdc.gov/nchs
/about/major/nsfg/abclist_d.htm.

Collum, Jason. "Reality Check Time Comes Before 'I Do.'" *American Family Association
Journal*, June 2003. Online: http://www.afajournal.org/2003/june/603marriage.asp.

DiCaro, Vincent. "NFI Releases Report on National Marriage Survey." *Fatherhood Today*
10, no. 3 (Summer 2005): 4–5.

Gutierrez, Mary A., and Glen Stimmel. "Management of and Counseling for Psychotropic
Drug-Induced Sexual Dysfunction." *Pharmacotherapy Publications* 19, no. 7 (1999):
823–831.

Hall, Carl T. "Study Speeds Up Biological Clocks—Fertility Rates Dip After Women Hit
27." *San Francisco Chronicle*, April 20, 2002, sec. A.

Isaacson, Walter. "The Heart Wants What It Wants." *Time*, August 31, 1992, Online: http:
//www.time.com/time/magazine/article/0,9171,976345-5,00.html.

Jayson, Sharon. "Cohabitation is Replacing Dating." *USA Today*, July 17, 2005, sec. L.

Margolis, Jonathan. *O: The Intimate History of the Orgasm*. New Delhi, India: Century
Publishers, 2004. Edited extract Online: http://www.sensualism.com/sex/orgasmic
.html.

Merriam-Webster's Online Dictionary. "Monogamy." Online: http://www.merriam-webster
.com/dictionary/.

Sloan, Carrie. "Cohabitation Nation." *Marie Claire* 14, no. 3 (March 2007): 106–113.

Vanilla Sky. Film. Directed by Cameron Crowe. Hollywood, CA: Paramount Pictures,
2001.

Wikipedia. "Common-law marriage." Online: http://en.wikipedia.org/wiki/Common-law
_marriage.